WILLIAM P. LYONS MASTER'S ESSAY AWARD

The William P. Lyons Master's Essay Award was established in 1960 by the Department of History of Loyola University, Chicago, and the Loyola University Press. The Award is made annually to encourage significant work at the Master's level in history in American universities. It recognizes scholarship that is exemplary in style and method, based solidly on original sources and interpretatively significant in current research.

STAUGHTON LYND

Anti-Federalism in Dutchess County, New York

A study of democracy and class conflict in the Revolutionary era

LOYOLA UNIVERSITY PRESS

Chicago, Illinois

1962

© 1962 Loyola University Press

Printed in the United States of America
Library of Congress Catalog Card Number: 62-18101

PREFACE

I should like to thank the following persons for reading all or part of the manuscript of this book, or discussing the material with me: my teachers, Professors Richard Morris and Harold Syrett of Columbia University; Professor Alfred Young of Paterson State College, New Jersey; Professor Milton Klein of Long Island University; Dr. Lee Benson of the Institute for Applied Social Research, Columbia University; Mr. Robert Christen of Manhattan College; and Mr. Robin Brooks of Rochester University.

Chapter 4 appeared in somewhat different form in the *William and Mary Quarterly* for July 1961.

In quoting from manuscripts, I have modernized capitalization, punctuation, and spelling, except where the original form of the document seemed to add significantly to its meaning.

STAUGHTON LYND

Columbia University

v

CONTENTS

FIGURES

INTRODUCTION

A few words need saying at the outset, first, to justify the restriction of this study to so small an area as a single county, and second, to explain the sense in which the interpretation here advanced is "economic."

Amid the cut and thrust of controversy over the origins of the United States Constitution, one thing agreed on by all combatants is the need for more detailed, local research. Beard himself recognized that "not even a beginning" had been made on the "enormous and laborious researches" required either to prove or disprove his interpretation; he said of his own pioneering pages that they merely sketched "the broad outlines of the study

1

which must be filled in and corrected by detailed investigations."[1] The recent critics of Beard[2] rightly charge that, after the publication of *An Economic Interpretation of the Constitution of the United States*, he did not go on to the close-in study his book advised. Yet these same critics have not been content themselves to dig in at the state, county, and township level, postponing continental synthesis to a later day. In their preoccupation with refuting Beard, Brown and McDonald were obliged to follow him in casting their analytical nets widely across all thirteen states; inevitably, the mesh was too coarse and even some of the big fish got away.[3] And so, despite the admonitions of the revisionists, research is still spread too wide and thin, and the patient work of building from the bottom up has hardly begun.

If the need for local research on this subject is granted, the choice of so small an area as a single county remains to be defended. The reason is simply that because voting returns for this period are (save for the New England states) rarely available for political units smaller than the county, counties are commonly assumed to have been homogeneous in sentiment. The mapping method of Turner and Libby, showing one county all one color and a second all another, does violence to the facts. For instance, because New York's upriver counties elected delegates to the ratifying convention who were all Anti-Federalist and because the counties near New York City elected either Federalists or (with one exception) Anti-Federalists who voted for ratification, Libby concluded that "New York presents the problem in its simplest form."[4] Yet one of the outstanding Federalist leaders, Chancellor Livingston, was the lord of Livingston Manor in the supposedly Anti-Federalist North, while Anti-Federalist propaganda was disseminated throughout the state and nation by John Lamb and his associates in New York City. If the present study demonstrates any one thing, it is that a sharp division of opinion existed within Dutchess County. Nor did this division originate in the fall of 1787. The arguments men used

2

in debating the Constitution, the allies they reached out to, were the fruit of a local struggle which went back farther than the impost battle, farther even than the debate on independence.

Naturally, the local historian must resist the temptation of concluding that the particular area he has chosen to investigate contains the key to the question at issue. Interesting as the Dutchess material is, it may be quite secondary in importance to that of Albany or Suffolk in clarifying the ratification struggle in New York. Moreover, the quasi-manorial character of Hudson Valley land tenure was unique in the United States; it is, therefore, particularly dangerous to reason by analogy from the events in Dutchess County.

Yet when evidence from a given locality is altogether at variance with conclusions assumed to hold generally true, it takes on special significance. And such is the bearing of the Dutchess material on the present tendency to minimize the conflict between economic classes as a factor in shaping the politics of the seventeen-eighties.[5]

A particular target of this revisionist tendency is the belief that a continuing struggle for class domination underlay the debate over independence, the conduct of the Revolution, the state politics of the Confederation period, the contest over the Constitution, and the rise of the Federalist and Republican parties in the seventeen-nineties. Advanced just before the First World War by Carl Becker[6] as well as by Beard, the concept of continuing class conflict colored the writing of American history for a generation. While Beard argued that the Constitution was designed to advance the interests and secure the power of one segment of society, Becker suggested that many of the moneyed and mercantile men who reaped an economic harvest from independence had been laggard Whigs or outright Tories. As Beard and Becker saw it, a radical group comprising frontier farmers and artisans achieved a short-lived ascendancy after 1776, reflected in the democratic nature of the early state constitutions; but the United

States Constitution sealed a victorious counterrevolution of the well-to-do. In rebuttal, the Handlins stated that in Massachusetts

> The groupings which emerged from these issues were not simple. Most important, the groupings on any one issue were not coterminous with those on another. Certainly there were not two clear-cut camps. . . . The mossy conception of two-party continuity, smooth-seeming and attractive at first sight, has preempted the most fertile areas of our thinking and prevented the growth of more fruitful interpretations.[7]

Among prominent students today, perhaps only Merrill Jensen[8] continues to uphold the essential features of the Beard and Becker view.

The present study demonstrates that in Dutchess County, New York, the Revolution was indeed—in Becker's famous phrase—a struggle as to who should rule at home as well as a struggle for home rule. The same economic groups, to a striking extent the same leaders, confronted each other in the tenants' rising of 1766, in the struggle during the Revolution over the confiscation and sale of Loyalist lands, and in the battle over ratification of the Constitution. The nature of the contending groups was unquestionably grounded in different degrees of access to the ownership of land; and since a freehold in land carried the suffrage with it, the political balance of power varied directly with changes in the distribution of land. The Dutchess Federalist leaders were closely tied to the largest landlords and old aristocratic families. The Anti-Federalist leaders to a man were middling gentry and *nouveau riche* businessmen. Thus, the evidence from Dutchess does not support McDonald's conclusion that

> the dynamic groups favoring and opposing the Constitution were essentially noneconomic groups struggling for political power, who sought and received support primarily through appeals to the economic self-interest of the voters . . .[9]

Rather, the political factions in Dutchess County had a well-defined economic basis.

4

This interpretation is economic. But it differs from Beard's in that it stresses not so much the economic gains and losses which the Constitution seemed to offer its individual promoters and critics, as it does the struggle for power between contending economic groups. Both Beard and his critics too often regard economic interests as so many disparate calculations of monetary gain and loss. So they are, perhaps, in a stable political situation where legislation centers on the allocation of a pork barrel of discrete economic advantages among different claimants. But the adoption of the United States Constitution was the settlement of a revolution. What was at stake was more than the realization of speculative windfalls in government securities, more even than a form of government: It was the answer to the question, on which group in society would the political center of gravity come to rest. Such, at least, is the interpretation suggested by the conflict in Dutchess County.

While the Dutchess evidence on the whole confirms Beard and Becker rather than their critics, it also suggests some qualifications of the Beard and Becker viewpoint.

First, it does not seem to be true that the Dutchess Federalists had been less ardent for independence, or less active in the war with England, than their Anti-Federalist antagonists. The division over the Constitution appears instead to be a split of the former Whig party into radical and conservative wings.

Second, Beard placed disproportionate emphasis upon the individual delegates at the Philadelphia and ratifying conventions, and tended to forget that a politician often represents a constituency without at the same time typifying it. To appreciate this, one has only to think of Dutchess's most celebrated gift to American history, Franklin Delano Roosevelt. In Lee Benson's words, Beard committed "the logical fallacy of regarding members of public assemblies as the electorate in microcosm."[10]

The importance of distinguishing between leaders and voters may be illustrated from recent work on Virginia. In 1953, Robert

Thomas showed that "the leaders of both the Federalist and Anti-Federalist parties came from the *same* class—slaveowners, large landowners, land speculators, army officers and professional people, in short, the gentry"; he concluded:

> The leaders of both parties were recruited from the same class, and the contest over ratification of the Federal Constitution in Virginia was essentially a struggle between competing groups within the aristocracy.[11]

Now, the second half of this conclusion simply does not follow from the first. Two quite different constituencies, with quite different objectives, might well have sent to the Virginia convention delegates similar in their economic and social standing. In 1955, Jackson Main argued that this indeed had been the case. He surveyed the economic characteristics of the county constituencies more extensively than had Thomas, and correlated this information with the voting records of the Virginia legislature in the seventeen-eighties. Main found that the typical Federalist county had many large landholdings, many tenants, and few medium-sized farms, while in the typical Anti-Federalist county middling farmers predominated. This contrast—which, incidentally, closely resembles the distinction between Federalist and Anti-Federalist parts of Dutchess County—Main found systematically expressed in the votes of county delegates in the years before 1788 in the Virginia legislature.[12]

Recognition that the Anti-Federalist leaders were not necessarily typical of the voters who elected them has been too long delayed. It has seemed unnecessarily puzzling that the "radical leaders" of the Revolutionary era were so conservative, in apparent contradiction to the extremism of Shays' Rebellion or the New York tenant riots of 1766. Thus, Tom Paine wrote pamphlets for Robert Morris, Samuel Adams supported the conservative Massachusetts constitution of 1780, and George Clinton led the New York militia against Shays' Rebellion. Nor were the Anti-Federalists distinguished by the sweeping democratic ideol-

6

ogy of a John Lilburne.[13] A model has been lacking to explain the two seemingly contradictory sets of facts: undeniable radicalism in much of the Anti-Federalist electorate, equally undeniable conservatism in almost all of its leadership.

The Dutchess County material suggests such a model. There the interests of the Anti-Federalist leaders were not identical with those of their constituents. The former were a handful of men concentrated in one town (Poughkeepsie), closely related by family and economic ties, and themselves often land speculators, landlords, or agents for landlords; the latter included many tenants with a militant history of antilandlordism. Yet the Anti-Federalist leaders were economically and socially a cut below the great Federalist landlords, and they built their political careers on the exploitation of tenant grievances. In a word, they acted not like revolutionists but like reform politicians; once independence was achieved, they sought no fundamental overturn, but greater elbow room for new men on the make.

These final qualifications rub some sharp edges off the moral dichotomy which students on both sides of the fence have sought to find in the struggle over the Constitution. At least in Dutchess County, the "Pro's" and "Anti's" cannot be differentiated by their "war records" in the Revolution; and while on the whole the Federalists were the party of wealth, there were rich politicians on both sides. Is it not likely that a final appreciation will discover some virtues in the Federalists, other virtues in their opponents: political wisdom, for instance, on the one hand, and a responsiveness to popular sentiment on the other? Perhaps only then will discussion of the Constitution escape sterile invocation of the forces of light in opposition to the forces of darkness and find that the adoption of the Constitution, like most historical events, destroyed some good things as it created others.

Dutchess County lies on the east bank of the Hudson River about halfway between New York City and Albany. In the eighteenth century, Dutchess included the present Putnam County

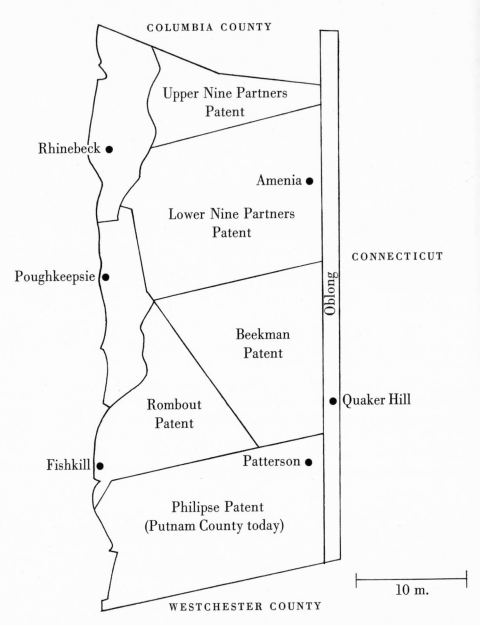

COLUMBIA COUNTY

Upper Nine Partners
Patent

Rhinebeck ●

Amenia ●

Lower Nine Partners
Patent

CONNECTICUT

Poughkeepsie ●

Oblong

Beekman
Patent

● Quaker Hill

Rombout
Patent

Fishkill ●

Patterson ●

Philipse Patent
(Putnam County today)

10 m.

WESTCHESTER COUNTY

Note: The political subdivisions of eighteenth-century Dutchess were called "pre-cincts." In general their boundaries followed those of the land patents.

FIGURE 1

Map of Dutchess County

(running from just above Peekskill on the south to just below Beacon on the north) and thus lay directly upriver from Westchester County. The county's eastern limit was the much-disputed boundary between New York and Connecticut, twenty miles of rugged travel from the Hudson.

From about 1725 to the end of the century, Dutchess County was the most rapidly expanding part of New York State. In 1731, Dutchess was New York's least populous county with 1,727 inhabitants. By 1756 the county's population was 13,289 (plus 859 Negro slaves), second only to that of Albany; in that year the historian William Smith wrote of Dutchess:

> The south part of the county is mountainous and fit only for iron works, but the rest contains a quantity of good upland well watered. The only villages in it are Poughkeepsie and the Fish Kill, though they scarce deserve the name. The inhabitants on the banks of the river are Dutch, but those more easterly, Englishmen, and, for the most part, emigrants from Connecticut and Long Island. There is no episcopal church in it. The growth of this county has been very sudden, and commenced but a few years ago. Within the memory of persons now living, it did not contain above twelve families; and, according to the latest returns of the militia, it will furnish at present, above 2500 fighting men.[14]

By 1790 the county population was 45,266 (including 1,856 Negro slaves), the white males over sixteen numbering 10,968.[15]

In the political geography of New York in the seventeen-eighties, Dutchess County lay between the northern counties, which regularly supported Governor George Clinton, and the counties near New York City, over which Hamilton and his associates gained increasing sway. Indicative of this intermediate position was the fact that Dutchess elected seven avowedly Anti-Federalist delegates to the Poughkeepsie ratifying convention, but four of them—including the principal Anti-Federalist spokesman, Melancton Smith—voted in the end for ratification. Had they not changed their votes, New York would not have ratified the Constitution in the summer of 1788.

9

THE ELECTION CAMPAIGN

OF 1788

Gentlemen out of doors should not be hasty in condemning a
system which probably rests on more good reasons than they are
aware of, especially when formed under such advantages, and
recommended by so many men of distinguished worth and abilities.
John Jay, Address to the People of the State of New York

The hands of the people without doors laid the foundation
of this revolution; their hands ought also to finish it.
Joseph Hawley to the Massachusetts Constitutional Convention, 1780

As the hot summer of 1788 drew to a close, the Philadelphia Constitutional Convention presented its handiwork to the
people at large and the theater of conflict shifted to the thirteen
states. In New York it was already clear that Governor George
Clinton would marshall his formidable influence against the proposed instrument. Clinton's brother-in-law, Peter Tappen, wrote
to him from Poughkeepsie on September 29:

> I find the new Constitution circulating here. It has but few warm
> friends here. William Kent, Doctor Thomas and Billings but the
> influence of the last will not do it much good. I am happy Judge Platt
> opposes it warmly. I make no doubt but that the common people here

will generally oppose it. I should think that the northern part of the county will be for adopting it. I judge from the leading men. I am fearful that the many publications in favor will injure as none publish against. I shall use my influence as far as I can and I hope I have some here.[1]

Four days later Dutchess County's only newspaper, the *Country Journal and Poughkeepsie Advertiser,* acknowledged the opening of the great debate by changing the inscription on its masthead. The prosaic message, "Advertisements of no more length than breadth, are inserted three weeks, for one dollar; and for every week after, one shilling and sixpence: longer ones in proportion," gave way to the poetic motto:

> In my free page let different works reside,
> Tho' party's hostile lines those works divide;
> Party! whose murdering spirit I abhor
> More subtly cruel, and less brave than war.[2]

Fortunately for the historian, Editor Powers was true to his word and printed lengthy polemics on both sides in his weekly issues through the months that followed. Condensed versions of some of the essays of "Publius" were also included with the paper as special supplements.

Discussions of the proposed Constitution in the *Country Journal* began with the publication on October 24, 1787, of the inflammatory address delivered to the New York members of the Cincinnati the preceding July 4 by Chancellor Robert R. Livingston. In this address Livingston posed the dichotomy between aristocracy and democracy which was to be the overriding theme of the ratification debate in Dutchess County and in the New York ratifying convention. "Can it be believed," Livingston asked his fellow officers,

> that an enlightened people think the science of government level to the meanest capacity? . . . Is it [not] well known that in some states the competence which affords leisure to attend to the affairs of government even in the hands of men who have risked their all for the establishment of freedom is urged by some as sufficient cause

for their not sharing in the administration of the country? . . . You are not formed to follow the lead of those you despise.

Coming from a great landlord whose mother, Margaret Beekman Livingston, owned 240,000 acres in Dutchess and six houses in the town of Rhinebeck, and whose father, Judge Robert Livingston, had been rejected as an Assembly representative for Dutchess in the bitter elections of 1768 and 1769, these words must have had special meaning for the farmers of Dutchess County. The Anti-Federalists, as in the pamphlet by Melancton Smith signed "A Plebeian," took pains to keep the issue as defined by Livingston before the voters' eyes.

The newspaper debate on the Constitution picked up tempo after February 1788, when Egbert Benson, a Dutchess representative in the state Assembly, carried a motion to call a New York ratifying convention. Between March 4, when the first nominations for Dutchess delegates to the convention appeared in the *Country Journal*, and April 29, the day of the election, more than twenty items dealing with the Constitution appeared in the newspaper. In previous years the election season had produced only a handful of mild and abstract injunctions to elect good men.

The newspaper war in the *Country Journal* must have been widely read throughout the county. In those days the newspaper was the basic printed source of public information and a citizen could ill afford to miss an issue. Here he found the text of the laws passed by the state legislature; here legal notice was given of bankruptcy sales; here, too, nominations for public office were announced by the candidates' backers. Although there was no postal or stage service to hamlets on the Connecticut border like Amenia,[3] by horseback or goods wagon the newspaper got through and the "Constitutional Society" of Amenia sent in pieces to the *Country Journal*.

Newspaper columns were supplemented by pamphlets. James Kent and Egbert Benson, leading Dutchess Federalists, circulated the *Federalist Papers* and John Jay's *Address to the People*

12

of the State of New York; in June 1788, after the Federalist defeat at the polls, an anonymous correspondent in the *Country Journal* asserted that, had Jay's essay been more widely distributed, his party would have made a stronger showing.[4] On the Anti-Federalist side, John Lamb sent up from New York City over three hundred copies of the *Centinel* and the *Columbian Patriot*, which were distributed by Peter Tappen, Lewis DuBois, and Theodorus Bailey in the western part of the county, and by Mathew Patterson in the east.[5]

This barrage of printed matter notwithstanding, the number of men who read the proposed Constitution before voting for or against it may have been quite small. In April, only three weeks before the election, the *Country Journal* printed a delightful hypothetical debate between the Anti-Federalist "Squire Artifice" and an "inoffensive well meaning ignorant man." After some preliminary talk about the weather,

> the Squire, with seeming indifference, addressed me thus: Well my friend, what think you of this new government that is proposed to us; I told him that I knew very little about it, I had heard my neighbors talk of it, but neither they nor myself had ever read it, and for my part if I had read it, I doubted if I could fully understand it.[6]

Many a man must have been like this one, many a vote settled in talk over a rail fence between indifferent scholars.

Accounts of the popular debate in New York[7] have been largely drawn from the elegant articles, adorned with classical citations, which appeared in the press of New York City. This ornate style was not well-received upriver. The Albany Anti-Federalist Committee wrote to John Lamb that he had sent them "a well composed piece but in a style too sublime and florid for the common people in this part of the country."[8] The debate in the *Country Journal* has a homely, conversational tone. The New York City press presents the political science with which men rationalized the inarticulate major premises of ideology, but the provincial press gives a glimpse of the ideologies themselves.

In the columns of the *Country Journal*, Federalist satirists painted the tenets of their opponents in no uncertain strokes. A writer who signed himself "Anarchy" gave this advice for the choosing of Anti-Federalist candidates:

> By no means choose a man possessed of a large estate as he will make a very improper member, because every possessor of wealth wishes to keep it, and if so, will readily give his assent to any government calculated for the security of property; but on the other hand, a man embarrassed in his circumstances, will never consent to the establishing a government that will not open a door for the discharge of his debts some other way than paying them. Learning has ever been considered by all wise men, from the followers of Jack Cade down to the Ulster, Orange and Dutchess Anti-Federalists, to be the bane of republicanism, as it creates distinctions among men, who are made by nature equal, you therefore cannot be too cautious of men of education of every denomination.

In referring to Jack Cade, the Federalist wit quipped better than he knew; for like any New York Anti-Federalist, the Kentish followers of Cade in 1451 complained of "the great rulers of all the country the which embraceth their tenants and other people by force to choose other persons than the commons' will is."[9] The letter of "Anarchy" continued:

> It will be dangerous to choose an officer of the late army because by travel and an acquaintance with the world, he has extended his ideas of humanity and public utility over the union, when they ought to be confined to the precinct he is chosen from, however if he either resigned or was deranged before the war was over, it is probable that he is disgusted with the federal government, and therefore may make a good instrument in opposing of it. By no means choose a member of the Cincinnati . . . on the other hand choose a man either in a profitable office under the state government, or in expectation of being so, for if he is doing comfortably now, he will not wish a change.[10]

This picture of the Anti-Federalist as poor, indebted, and unlearned, hostile to rich men and officers, is amplified by the

14

versatile creator of "Squire Artifice," the fictional Anti-Federalist propagandist already encountered.

> The Squire said it was easy to understand that it was a plot to take away our religious and civil liberties, and make slaves of us; and on my asking why he thought so, he answered, that in the first place, the framers of the Constitution had acted without any authority, that they were usurpers, and deserved to be hanged, that the Constitution gave them as much power as the King of England ever had, that they were going to raise an army and billet them on the people, and tax the people to pay for both, that our taxes would be three times heavier than they now are, that all this was to be done to provide a place for the great men's sons, who would be appointed officers in the navy and army, and tax masters over the honest farmers, that the liberty of the press was taken away to prevent the people concerting any measures for the recovery of their liberties, that the trial by jury was taken away from us, and that every cause was to be determined by judges appointed by them to do as they ordered them, that our religion was taken away from us, and that popery, or no religion at all, would be established in its stead, that the impost that belonged to this State, was to be taken away from us, and to be divided among all the States.[11]

Especially interesting here is the explicit comparison of the Constitution with the pre-Revolutionary British administration, and the fact that so many of the grievances anticipated are those of the Declaration of Independence. As Merrill Jensen observes:

> The distrust of centralization, of government spread over a great area, was the product of both political theory and practical experience . . . Centralized government, with a legal veto on State laws, the power to enact general and uniform legislation, and the power to use arms to subdue rebellious social groups within the States, had disappeared with the Declaration of Independence.[12]

The Federalist characterization of Anti-Federalist attitudes was confirmed in its main lines by a curious exchange of letters regarding the nomination of Anti-Federalist Melancton Smith. Smith had lived in Dutchess for some twenty years before the Revolution. During the Revolution he served as sheriff, commissioner for detecting conspiracies, captain of the militia, judge, and contractor for the Army, amassing in the latter capacity a considerable fortune. In 1784 he moved to New York City and became a prominent merchant. Since the New York Anti-Federalists despaired of electing any delegates from New York City, Smith was one of the seven men nominated by the Dutchess Anti-Federalists in a caucus at Oswego on February 26.[13] As a delegate at the Poughkeepsie ratifying convention he was to be the leading Anti-Federalist spokesman and the key figure in the shift of enough Anti-Federalist votes to ensure New York's ratification. Smith's prominence makes the controversy about his nomination doubly interesting.

Smith's nomination was protested by a correspondent calling himself "One of Many." Whether the writer was as he claimed an Anti-Federalist, or whether as subsequent letters charged he was a Federalist seeking to split the Anti-Federalist voters, his remarks were intended to appeal to the Anti-Federalist voters; as such, they shed further light on Anti-Federalist beliefs. "One of Many" charged that Smith had been nominated by a caucus in which "the little overbearing precinct of Poughkeepsie" was overrepresented, and several other parts of the county were not represented at all. "What," he asked, "is the plain English in the nomination of Mr. Smith of New York . . . Must we call in the assistance of strangers and New York merchants?" "One of Many" then went on to make a strangely accurate prophecy about Smith's probable attitude as a convention delegate.

> It is said (and we apprehend the information may be relied on) that Mr. Smith has grown *cool* on the question, and that he considers the adoption of the new Constitution by Massachusetts, as decisive for the continent, and that it would be as fruitless as it would be inexpedient for this State, even if there should be a majority against it, to stand out against the general sense and ardent feelings of America. If this be the case, we would oppose such a delegate even if he lived in this county.[14]

"One of Many" was promptly answered by "Cassius" in a letter to "the opposers of the new Constitution in Dutchess County." What a delegate should have, according to this writer, was "character, firmness and ability," residence in the county being quite secondary.[15] These words inspired "A Landholder" to nominate six other New York City merchants together with Melancton Smith, and explain his farcical nomination thus:

> They are all, as you will perceive, merchants residing in the city of New York. This however, I take it can be no manner of objection, since the only requisite qualifications are *character, firmness and ability*, and since I have too much well grounded respect for the gentlemen who met a few weeks since in Beekman's precinct, to believe that we have suitable timber in our own county. . . . After we have got cleverly into the practice, I think we may as well as not get rid entirely of the whole burden of elections, and yet reap all their salutary blessings, by letting New York choose seven men for us as well as nine for themselves.[16]

These letters, with their localism and suspicion of merchants, round out a picture of the Anti-Federalist viewpoint in Dutchess County. Taken as a whole, the discussion in the *Country Journal* centered on a generalized contrast between, on the one hand, the "great men," and on the other, what "One of Many" called "the discerning and independent yeomanry of Dutchess," or alternatively, "the peaceable and industrious poor." Critics of Beard like Robert Brown[17] and Richard Hofstadter[18] have accused him of neglecting the words men used and forever seeking out hidden motives. But the words used about the Constitution in the *Country Journal* take for granted just the kind of struggle between broad group interests which Beard supposed: "between," as Beard put it, "substantial personalty interests on the one hand and the small farming and debtor interests on the other."[19] There remains the possibility, of course, that the social conflict perceived by contemporaries was not really there, or that they invoked this conflict as a stock rhetorical theme which falsified reality; exploration of this possibility will be the task of subsequent chapters.

The outpouring of newspaper polemics in Dutchess County was caused by something more than the intrinsic importance of the Constitutional issue. There were three special features of the election of April 1788 which made it more difficult than usual for landlords and party managers to "deliver" votes. These features were universal manhood suffrage, the secret ballot, and the creation of polling places in each town and precinct, rather than at the county seat alone.[20] Taken together, the three innovations in electoral procedure required a new kind of campaign, designed to produce by persuasion votes which personal influence could no longer control.

There is no precise way to calculate the effect of these measures, because voting statistics for the seventeen-eighties are so sketchy. Spaulding argues that universal manhood suffrage did not change the ratio in which votes were distributed between the two parties.[21] But this could not have been known in advance. And while we cannot say just how many men the freehold qualification had prevented from voting in Dutchess County before 1788,[22] there can be little doubt that a much higher percentage of the county's adult males voted in 1788 than in previous elections. For example, whereas in 1783 the poll list in Poughkeepsie numbered only 92[23] in an adult male population of at least 500,[24] in 1788 about 2,700 of 10,000 adult males in the county voted. These new voters may have been either persons previously disenfranchised, or persons who lived in the backcountry and had found the journey to Poughkeepsie prohibitive.[25] In either case, the new voters must have helped to call forth the flood of propaganda. As Becker puts it:

> The great families, the traditional leaders, found it necessary . . . to modify their methods of political management. . . . The personal relation, as a means of holding the voters in line, was replaced by appeals to the voters' intelligence or interest, in the form of public

18

letters or resolutions setting forth the principles for which the candidate stood.[26]

The uphill propaganda battle of the Dutchess Federalists did
not succeed. The *Country Journal* orators agreed that preelection
sentiment was overwhelmingly Anti-Federalist; and when the
April 29 election came, the Anti-Federalist candidates were
elected by a majority of roughly two to one. Almost all the voters
chose a "straight ticket"; the Anti-Federalist candidate with the
most votes received only 33 more votes that the Anti-Federalist
candidate with the least votes (1,765 and 1,732), and the figures
for the defeated Federalists were similar (892 and 854).[27] The
two-to-one ratio in Dutchess was typical of the state as a whole,
in which the Anti-Federalists elected forty-six delegates and the
Federalists nineteen. Well might James Hughes exult in a letter
to John Lamb that the "well born who are the leaders of that
party" had never been so threatened in their power.[28]

THE CANDIDATES

AND THEIR CONSTITUENCIES

A representative body, composed principally of respectable
yeomanry, is the best possible security to liberty.
Melancton Smith at the New York Ratifying Convention

Whom, in the name of common sense, will we have to represent
us? Why he [Smith] must go out into the highways, and pick up
the rogue and the robber; he must go to the hedges and ditches,
and bring in the poor, the blind and the lame.
Robert R. Livingston at the New York Ratifying Convention

Who were the Federalists and Anti-Federalists of Dutchess
County in 1788? Were the Anti-Federalists right when they
called themselves "yeomen" and their opponents "wellborn"?
With how much justice did the Federalists charge that New York
State officeholders made up the core of the Anti-Federalist party?
And to what extent did the division over the Constitution in
Dutchess correspond to other major political divisions in the
county between 1750 and 1800: tenant and landlord, Whig and
Tory, Jeffersonian and Hamiltonian?

These questions could be more readily answered if voting
statistics existed for the precincts into which Dutchess County

was divided. But neither the state librarian at Albany nor the county clerk at Poughkeepsie reports such records, which apparently were systematically preserved only from the seventeen-nineties. In the absence of this most desirable type of data, the argument must be more circumstantial. In this chapter, attention will be focused on the men who led the Federalist and Anti-Federalist parties in 1788; in the following two chapters, the focus will be on the alignment of political groups which grew out of the pre-Revolutionary struggle between tenants and landlords. In a word, our argument will be that this alignment persisted into the seventeen-eighties and seventeen-nineties, and went far in determining the answer to the question, "Which side are you on?" in 1788.

On the map (p. 22) are plotted the home neighborhoods of the seven Federalist and seven Anti-Federalist candidates for the New York ratifying convention, the four men who distributed Anti-Federalist literature in Dutchess County, and the three men who (in addition to Egbert Benson, a candidate) issued a call for a Federalist nominating caucus. Thus we have for each party seven candidates and a smaller group who might be called "party managers."

The map suggests strongly that the headquarters of the Dutchess Federalists was the northwest and that the headquarters of the Anti-Federalists was, as "One of Many" charged, "the little overbearing precinct of Poughkeepsie." Five of the eleven Anti-Federalists lived in Poughkeepsie. Five of the ten Federalists—or six, if we count Egbert Benson, who came from a Rhinebeck family[1]—lived along the east bank of the Hudson between Poughkeepsie and the Columbia County line.

What, then, was the character of the northwestern and Poughkeepsie neighborhoods in which the Federalist and Anti-Federalist leadership centered?

Northwest Dutchess was the home of most of the great absentee landowners of the eighteenth century, just as it was the

21

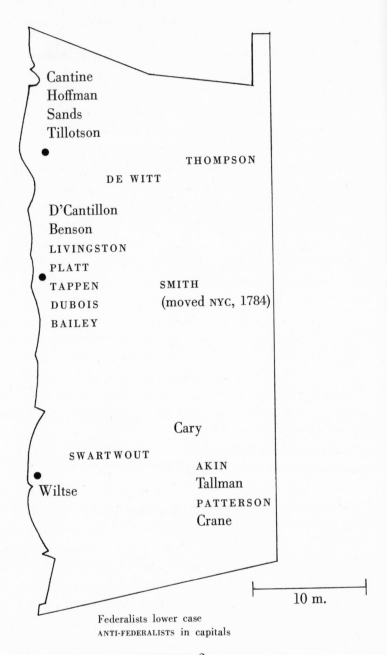

FIGURE 2

Map of Home Neighborhoods of Party Leaders

site of most of the "places" of the nineteenth-century gentry. Many of the great landlords were heirs of Henry Beekman, Sr. (1652-1716), whose holdings comprised most of Rhinebeck, Beekman, and Pawling precincts. He bequeathed his property in three equal parts to his daughters and to his son, Henry Beekman, Jr., who in the second quarter of the eighteenth century "ruled the rapidly growing population of Dutchess almost as if he had been its manor lord."[2] All three branches of the Beekman heirs married in the first or second generation into the Livingston family, one of the most powerful families in the province, whose vast holdings north of Dutchess County cast a formidable shadow of influence southward. Chancellor Robert R. Livingston, Jr., the heir of part of Margaret Beekman Livingston's 240,000 acres in Dutchess County,[3] was next to Hamilton the most prominent Federalist spokesman in the New York ratifying convention.

What Thorstein Veblen called the "underlying population" was in both Rhinebeck and Northeast precincts made up in good part of Palatine Germans. Their ancestors had been imported in the early eighteenth century as indentured servants and settled at Rhinebeck and just across the Hudson to extract tar from the pitch pine.[4] Richard Smith, traveling up the Hudson in 1769, landed at Henry Beekman's manor in Rhinebeck and found no one who could speak English; he noted that one tenant paid an annual rent of twenty bushels of wheat for his farm of ninety-seven acres and had the liberty to cut wood anywhere on the manor.[5] The quasi-feudal social atmosphere in these parts of the county is suggested by the Old Red Dutch Church, erected in northern Rhinebeck about the time of the Revolution.

> A raised floor extended along each side of the body of the house, on which were square pews, provided with an ornamental railing on top, so high that when a person was seated nothing of him was visible except his head. These were intended for the use of the families of the landed proprietors. The common people occupied the slips in

the body of the church. The elders and leading members sat in the side pews on either side of the pulpit.[6]

Probably typical of Rhinebeck leases were those customary in the seventeen-nineties at the estate of Morgan Lewis, a future governor of New York who married one of Chancellor Livingston's sisters. His leases were usually in perpetuity, thus providing both security of tenure and the legal status of freeholder. But they also customarily contained such features as:

> . . . a provision that the tenant should pay a certain proportion of the sale money, and this was usually from one-sixth to one-tenth; also to deliver a certain number of bushels of wheat, usually "good merchantable winter wheat"; also to do a certain number of days riding whenever he was directed to do it, and to furnish a few fowls, mentioned often as "fat fowls"; and to have his grain ground at Lewis' mill, providing it was within a certain number of miles of the mill.

A "day's riding" meant, in the terminology of one lease:

> . . . yielding, rendering and performing to said Morgan Lewis, his heirs and assigns, one day's work with wagon, sleigh or plow, two horses or oxen and an able man to drive in such manner with such of the above instruments and at such times and place, yearly and every year forever, within ten miles of the demised premises . . . as said Morgan Lewis . . . shall direct.[7]

Seventeen of the leases on this estate, incidentally, were still in full force in 1917.

Such was the character of the Federalist headquarters in Dutchess County. As the genealogical chart shows, two of our ten Federalists, Thomas Tillotson and Robert Sands, had married into the Beekman-Livingston clan. Two others of the ten, Peter Cantine and Richard D'Cantillon, were merchants, each with his own "landing." D'Cantillon acquired his landing— along with a store, mill, and ten-room house measuring forty-two by thirty feet—by marrying into the wealthy Stoutenburg family.[8] One of the members of this family, Jacobus Stoutenburg,

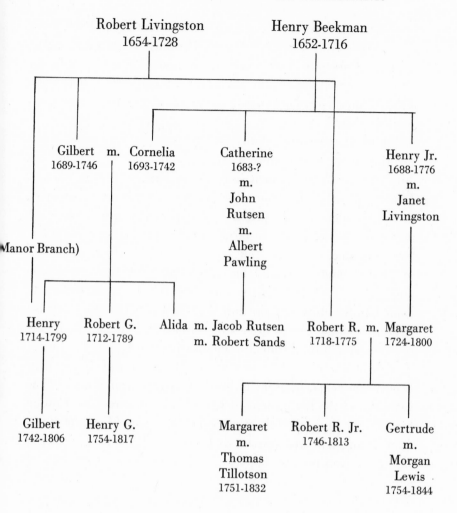

FIGURE 3

Diagram of Partial Genealogy of
Beekman and Livingston Families

Sources: Joan Gordon, "Kinship and Class: The Livingstons of New York"; Philip
White, *The Beekmans of New York*; James Smith, *History of Dutchess County*.

25

is believed to have owned 350 acres near the Hyde Park landing, 3,000 acres in eastern Clinton Precinct, seventy-five farms
between Rhinebeck and Poughkeepsie, and a "gore" (a holding,
often triangular, along the boundary of two larger holdings)
with its point on the Hudson River running east to the Connecticut line.[9]

Without the voting statistics, the historian cannot say with
certainty that northwestern Dutchess voted Federalist; he can
only say, as Peter Tappen said at the time to George Clinton
(above, p. 10), that since the leading men were Federalist,
their dependents would probably vote that way also. Where, as
in northwest Dutchess, the large landlords were resident rather
than absentee, there are few recorded instances in this period
of those tenants who had the vote[10] opposing their landlords
politically. Thus the Albany Anti-Federalist Committee wrote
John Lamb before the election that they expected to carry all
Albany County except Rensselaer Manor;[11] and early in the
seventeen-eighties a Dutchess landlord wrote his rent collector
that the Clintonians had passed a bill prohibiting leases over
twenty-one years, in order to prevent tenants from voting.[12] The
influence of the Livingstons of Clermont, just across the Columbia County line, was felt at election time when Margaret Beekman Livingston, who owned six houses in Rhinebeck, sent her
bailiff Cockburn to see her tenants.[13] Since the evidence clearly
suggests a firm relationship between the great landowning families of Dutchess County and the Dutchess Federalist leaders,
and since this part of the county was staunchly Federalist in
the seventeen-nineties,[14] it seems reasonable to suppose it was
Federalist in 1788 as well.

If in late eighteenth-century Dutchess, as in early nineteenth-
century Albany, Rensselaer, and Columbia counties, "the
wealthier of the old stock were Federalist," [15] the Anti-Federalist
leadership in and near Poughkeepsie was drawn from families
of moderate wealth. Many of these were Dutch families as long

resident in Dutchess as the Federalist Livingstons or Hoffmans; such were the clans of Tappen, Swartwout, and DeWitt.[16] Zephaniah Platt and Melancton Smith, on the other hand, had come to backcountry Dutchess from Long Island and moved to Poughkeepsie during the Revolutionary War. Gilbert Livingston belonged to a branch of the enormous Livingston tribe distinctly less rich and socially prominent than the manor Livingstons.

Widespread freehold tenure, rather than manorial estates, gave the Poughkeepsie neighborhood its economic tone. Yet by no stretch of the imagination were any of the Anti-Federalist candidates or managers impoverished yeomen. Zephaniah Platt was agent and manager for a speculative group which bought up 30,000 acres worth of claims to land which had been granted to soldiers in the Revolution in place of pay. The group that "by pushing their claims to the preference" obtained a patent for this site, which became the town of Plattsburgh, included Dutchess Anti-Federalists Melancton Smith, Jacobus Swartwout, and Peter Tappen, and downstate Anti-Federalists Thomas Tredwell and Jonathan Lawrence.[17] The law practice of Gilbert Livingston and his partner, the Federalist James Kent, consisted in good part of prosecutions for the collection of debts.[18] Moreover, Gilbert Livingston acted as agent for his uncle Robert Gilbert Livingston, heir to one third of Henry Beekman's vast holdings.

> Robert Gilbert's instructions to his nephew regarding these lands show great resoluteness about the collection of back rents, eviction of tenants, and the protection of his property from the destructiveness of the tenants. His references to his tenants generally indicate a disregard for them and the need to make his authority and superior position known. "By no means let him stay on the place. Drive him off as soon as possible. I would rather the farm should stand idle than suffer such a sot to stay on it."[19]

In addition to what Kent called a "great and established run of business" as a lawyer, Gilbert Livingston had at least £7,540 worth of real estate.[20]

The Anti-Federalist leaders outside Poughkeepsie were also men of substance. Jacobus Swartwout held £7,372 in New York State securities, along with $283 in continentals.[21] Ezra Thompson was a "fairly prosperous farmer"[22] whose family owned at least 2,400 acres in the Amenia region.[23] John DeWitt owned and operated a Clinton grist mill for twenty-seven years.[24] Jonathan Akin was a patriarchal Quaker landlord. In his home

> a north door, which commanded the pleasant outlook, was opened at May-time and closed only at night until Autumn; where every one, high and low, felt an equal right to enter, and received the same welcome.[25]

It is instructive to compare the tax assessments of the Poughkeepsie Anti-Federalist leaders with the assessments in the south Dutchess precincts (the area which later became Putnam County), where the most radical tenants lived. In 1771, Zephaniah Platt was assessed for £16, John Bailey for £13, Gilbert Livingston and Lewis DuBois for £5; the highest Poughkeepsie assessment was £38.[26] In 1777 in southern Dutchess, 727 of 765 taxpayers were rated at £4 or less; 28 were rated from £5 to £9; and 9 were rated at £10 or more. One of the three landlords of this south Dutchess land, Beverly Robinson, was rated at £70.[27] Clearly, these figures confirm the impression that the Anti-Federalist leaders were a long step up the social ladder from their constituents, yet still well below the Federalist landlords.

Melancton Smith, as a resident of New York City, is rather a separate case. Besides running a mercantile establishment, he speculated heavily in confiscated Loyalist lands and in the complex and shady schemes of William Duer, who was to become Hamilton's undersecretary of the treasury.[28] He was indeed almost a caricature of a man identified with "personalty." No wonder that those Anti-Federalists for whom "One of Many" spoke (or to whom he appealed) were suspicious of Smith.

These Anti-Federalist leaders were bound together by an extraordinary network of family and economic ties, as the dia-

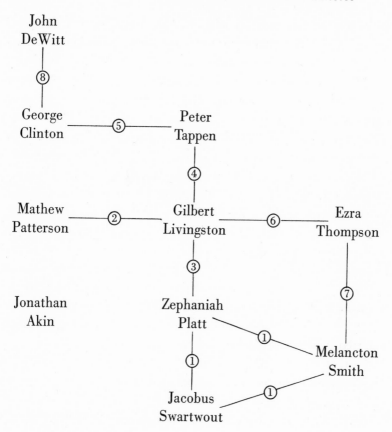

1 Platt, Smith, and Swartwout were proprietors of the Plattsburgh speculation.
2 Patterson's daughter married Livingston's brother.
3 Platt's son married Livingston's sister.
4 Tappen, Livingston, and Smith's brother ran a general mercantile business in Poughkeepsie. Tappen and Livingston were brothers-in-law.
5 Clinton and Tappen were brothers-in-law.
6 Thompson's son married Livingston's daughter and became Livingston's law partner.
7 Smith and Thompson were brothers-in-law.
8 Clinton's brother James married a DeWitt.

FIGURE 4

Diagram of Some Family and Economic Ties Among Dutchess County Anti-Federalists

gram shows. For example, Israel Smith, brother of Melancton Smith, ran a general merchandise business with Peter Tappen and his brother-in-law, Gilbert Livingston; through his sister Rachel, he was also a brother-in-law of Ezra Thompson, whose son, Smith Thompson—who was to become secretary of the Navy under Monroe—in turn married Gilbert Livingston's daughter.[29] Through Tappen, DeWitt, and Livingston, the Dutchess Anti-Federalists were related to George Clinton. Furthermore, this generation of Anti-Federalist leaders was also connected through marriage to the leaders of the antilandlord party in Dutchess before the Revolution, Leonard Van Kleek and Dirck Brinckerhoff. For Jacobus Swartwout married one of the Brinckerhoffs[30] and Gilbert Livingston's father-in-law married a sister of Leonard Van Kleek.[31]

It is true that there were certain business and kinship ties between the Federalist and Anti-Federalist leaders. Thus, Kent's sister Hannah married into the Platt family,[32] and Kent himself married a sister of Bailey.[33] Anti-Federalist Peter Tappen and Federalist Richard D'Cantillon were partners in "the Stocking Manufactory" in Clinton.[34] But the density of these "exogamous" bonds was far less than the density of ties within each of the leadership cliques. The cross-ties hardly justify Milton Klein's revision of Becker, that "family ties served less to clarify the lines of political divergence than to obscure them."[35]

But while recognizing the party leaders as "interests," in the sense made notorious by Sir Lewis Namier, it would be wrong to conclude with Namier that these little knots of mutually dependent politicians represented no interests other than their own. Where county gentry like Platt or Swartwout could make common cause with the genuine yeomen who elected them was in mutual opposition to the great landlords of the Beekman-Livingston connection. While the Anti-Federalist leaders were no humble yeomen, they were by no means the social or economic equals of the Beekman-Livingston Federalist group.

The relation of Gilbert Livingston to his Livingston relatives demonstrates this clearly. No doubt many readers of the debates in the New York ratifying convention have been puzzled by the fact that the sharpest recorded exchanges were between two Livingstons, Gilbert and Chancellor Robert. The explanation lies in the fact that the chancellor was the scion of the Clermont branch of the family, to which a part of the Livingston property descended, whereas Gilbert belonged to a nonpropertied branch of distinctly inferior status. Gilbert (1742-1806) was the grandson of the first Gilbert (1689-1746), one of three sons of the original Robert Livingston. No descendant of this first Gilbert Livingston "became a landlord or planter or gentleman. This is not surprising in that the former required great real property and the latter great personal property."[36] Whereas for the manor and Clermont Livingstons politics was an avocation, "for the Gilbert line . . . local public offices tended to be a means of livelihood."[37] Thus, Gilbert's father, Henry (1714-1799), was for most of his adult life Dutchess' county clerk, the same position from which, in Ulster, George Clinton began his political career. The clerkship descending to one of Gilbert's brothers, Gilbert usually occupied the office of surrogate, becoming clerk only in the last two years of his life, 1804-1806.[38]

No such differences existed between the backcountry candidates of the two parties. In this part of the county the typical candidate, whether Federalist or Anti-Federalist, was a country squire who might work with his hands and might be the tenant of an absentee landlord. Henry Luddington did not become owner of his 229 acres until 1812.[39] Luddington and Joseph Crane, another Federalist candidate, were both rated at only four pounds in 1777, their Anti-Federalist opponent, Mathew Patterson, at three pounds.[40] But such relatively humble circumstances did not prevent Crane and Luddington from spending frequent social evenings with their Westchester Federalist neighbor, John Jay.[41]

Just north of this group of men, in southern Beekman Precinct, lived the Federalist candidate Dr. Ebeneezer Cary and his near neighbor, James Vanderburgh. Vanderburgh was such an ardent Federalist that he named one son George Washington and another Federal.[42] Apparently somewhat more affluent than Crane and Luddington, Vanderburgh owned nine hundred acres in Beekman and another nine hundred acres elsewhere.[43] He was, however, of the same stamp of patriarchal country gentleman as the Anti-Federalist Jonathan Akin, into whose family two of Vanderburgh's children married.[44] Vanderburgh, who like many prosperous farmers ran a country store, was noted for carrying his more indigent neighbors' accounts through the winter months. As a militia colonel during the Revolution, he once let his men go home to get the spring seed in and paid a thousand-dollar fine for his generosity. On the other hand, when one of his sons killed a Negro slave boy, "nothing was done about it."[45]

The difference in social atmosphere between this southeastern part of the county and the northwest was extreme. To the Old Red Dutch Church of Rhinebeck we can contrast the Baptist congregation of Patterson which split in 1796 "on account of the superflous dress, and the holding of posts of civil and military office in earthly states, by certain members."[46] While slaveholding was common here as in all parts of Dutchess County in 1788, the Quakers of Pawling were one of the first organized groups in the country to exclude members who held slaves,[47] and Baptist groups along the eastern frontier also occasionally declared against the practice.[48] Political personalities, however, were not often so extreme. Neither Federalist Henry Luddington nor Anti-Federalist Mathew Patterson were Baptists, but rather trustees of the more respectable Patterson Presbyterian Church.[49]

Although the backcountry candidates of the two parties were similar in socio-economic status, yet the southeastern backcountry was a distinctly Anti-Federalist constituency. Again, in the absence of precinct voting statistics, the evidence is circumstantial but cumulatively convincing. As the next two chapters will show, southeastern Dutchess had a long and sometimes bloody history of antilandlordism. In 1785 a meeting of Amenia free-holders inserted in the *Country Journal* a characteristically Clin-tonian program for paper money, nonpayment of debts to Tories, and subdivision of electoral districts.[50] And in the seven-teen-nineties, as previously noted, when northern Dutchess was consistently Federalist and central Dutchess wavered, the south was Jeffersonian; finally, in 1812, this section left the rest of the county altogether.

If not all Federalists were wellborn, as the Anti-Federalists implied, the Federalists were equally mistaken in inferring that most of their opponents were state officeholders. Gilbert Living-ston might be surrogate of Dutchess County, but Egbert Benson was attorney general of New York State. Anti-Federalists Zeph-aniah Platt and Jacobus Swartwout had each served two terms on the Council of Appointment since the Revolution, but in Janu-ary 1788, Federalist Anthony Hoffman had entered the Coun-cil.[51] Evidently Federalists were as often appointed judges and justices of the peace as were Anti-Federalists. In the southeast, for example, Federalists Joseph Crane, Henry Luddington, and James Vanderburgh held judicial posts along with Anti-Feder-alists Jonathan Akin and Mathew Patterson.[52] This is not to deny that Anti-Federalists enjoyed the lion's share of Clintonian pa-tronage during the seventeen-eighties. Zephaniah Platt had held the key post of first judge of the county courts since 1781,[53] and Dutchess sheriffs after the Revolution were all from the Anti-Federalist group.[54] The point is, rather, that not one of the lead-ing Dutchess Anti-Federalists appears to have derived the bulk of his income from political office, while Dutchess Federalists enjoyed a substantial if minority share of the patronage.

Turning from appointive to elective offices, one finds that Dutchess Federalists were elected surprisingly often during the decade between the outbreak of the Revolution and the adoption of the Constitution. Whether one examines the provincial congresses of the early war years, the Senate, the Assembly, or the Continental Congress,[55] one finds men who were Federalists in 1788 as well as men who were Anti-Federalists. As a matter of fact, the seven men elected from Dutchess to the Assembly in 1787 included three who were Federalists in 1788 and only two who were Anti-Federalists.[56]

An astonishing number of the leaders in both Dutchess parties had held the position of precinct supervisor sometime before 1788. Seven of the eleven Anti-Federalists and seven of the ten Federalists had occupied the office, the equality demonstrating again that the Dutchess Federalists were hardly political pariahs before 1788.[57] Supervisors, moreover, are always described as being elected by "the Freeholders and Inhabitants" of a given precinct, in other words by the same universal manhood suffrage introduced in 1788 in the election of the ratifying convention;[58] voting, however, was probably *viva voce* or by show of hands rather than by secret ballot.[59] The supervisor received three shilling a day[60] and, as his title suggests, overlooked the work of the tax assessors, constables, overseers of highways, and other minor local officials. The wealthiest landowners often held these offices,[61] which evidently carried with them the overall responsibility for neighborhood affairs exercised in England by the justice of the peace.

Thus most of the candidates in 1788 could have made the assertion of the "inoffensive well meaning ignorant man":

> As my manner is to treat every body with civility, the people suppose me to be a well disposed civil man; I have been elected several times in the course of my life to the offices of poor-master, road-master, etc., and as I have acted as well as I knew how in them, I am supposed to have some small influence among my neighbors under that opinion.[62]

The political prominence of Federalists in Dutchess from the Revolution to 1788 suggests that, contrary to another Anti-

Federalist stereotype, the Federalists may have been Whigs rather than Tories. And so indeed it was. Egbert Benson was chairman of the Dutchess Committee of Safety and the associate of Anti-Federalists Smith, Tappen, Livingston, Platt, and Swartwout on numerous committees to detect Tory conspiracies.[63] Ebeneezer Cary was an adjutant, and D'Cantillon and Tallman majors, in the Dutchess militia.[64] Thomas Tillotson was a surgeon in the Revolutionary Army. All the Cranes were fervent Whigs, and Joseph Crane was chairman of the Southeast Precinct Committee of Safety.[65]

These facts require the revision of one of the Becker-Beard assumptions. The Federalists of 1788 were not the Tories of 1777 in new guise. Rather, they were the conservative wing of a Whig party which, having won independence, divided over how independence should be used.

In summary, a survey of the Dutchess candidates and their constituencies suggests a pattern made up of three socio-economic groups. The largest landlords and the oldest aristocratic families, with their tenant and professional dependents, were Federalists. This group was strongest in the northern part of the county. The well-established freeholders, the county gentry with moderate incomes and immoderate ambitions, were Anti- Federalist. This group centered in central Dutchess, in the Poughkeepsie neighborhood. The contrasting economic characters of the two neighborhoods are strikingly similar to those Jackson Main has found in Virginia. Northern Virginia, Main writes,

> had been from the beginning an enormous speculative enterprise, in which the landowners profited by rentals rather than by sales, and although by the 1780's there were a large number of landowners, much of the area was still controlled by a relatively few families who had a large number of tenants.

In the North there was

> a small middle class, an above-average number of the lesser farmers, a very high percentage of tenants, and a wealthy aristocracy which

controlled a considerable part of the property. Since only those with land could vote, the political influence of the few could be exerted in proportion to their economic power.

The Southside had opposite characteristics. Nearly half of the adult males had land, and there were far fewer tenants; the number of medium-sized farms was much greater, and there were fewer of the small; large estates existed, but the land and other property was more equally divided, so that the economic power of the great planters was much reduced.[66]

Thus, in Dutchess as in Virginia, while the delegates of both parties to the ratifying convention can be broadly described as "gentry," this word encompasses some definite subgroupings. What might be called the greater gentry went, with its economic retinue, Federalist; opposing it was a lesser gentry which, in its resentment of the very great, liked to call itself a humble, honest, independent, and respectable yeomanry.[67]

These self-styled yeomen were politically supported by a third group, the more genuine yeomanry of the interior. This was the constituency which the well-to-do Poughkeepsie politicians represented. The next two chapters will tell how these politicians rose to power in the seventeen-sixties by making political capital of yeoman and tenant discontent; how during the Revolution this discontent forced the sale of Loyalist lands and, in so doing, broke the Whig coalition into radical and conservative wings; and how, therefore, in this generation-long struggle the battle lines of 1788 were formed.

THE TENANT RISING OF 1766

AND THE ORIGIN

OF PARTY CONFLICT

By what information I could collect from the inhabitants,
those of the Nine Partners are a riotous people and Levellers
by principle.
Sergeant Cassidy of the British Army, 1771

There is no law for poor men.
Testimony at the trial of William Prendergast, 1766

Dutchess County before the American Revolution was not
the mellow and genteel community we know today. It was a
society in which an heiress married "under a crimson canopy
emblazoned with the family crest in gold—a demi-lion crowned
issuing from a coronet"; and "as on rent day, the tenants gathered before the manor hall to feast and wish happiness to the
bride while within a lavish banquet was spread for the Van Cort-
landts, Livingstons and other river families."[1] It was a society,
too, in which the leader of a tenant rising was sentenced to be
hanged, drawn, and quartered for high treason: that is, to be
hung, cut down, and have his severed genitals and extracted

intestines burnt before his eyes while he was (in theory at least) still alive.[2]

The brilliance and brutality of this neofeudal society rested on the ownership of land. By 1710, when the population of Dutchess numbered only a hundred-odd families,[3] every one of the county's eight hundred square miles had been patented to a few dozen absentee landlords; and in the seventeen-eighties, Dutchess, of all New York's counties, still "showed the proudest array of large, well-settled patents."[4] Between tenant and landlord, as between mortar and pestle, the politics of the county was formed. "If one may judge anything by the number and nature of the cases in Dutchess County courts," comments McCracken, "the period of the Revolution witnessed a conflict in society beginning twenty years earlier and lasting ten years longer than the actual hostilities of war."[5] The struggle between landlord and tenant in Dutchess flared into armed riots in the seventeen-sixties; was fundamentally settled by the sequestration and sale of the Morris and Robinson holdings in the Revolution; but lingered on, in many individual dramas of mortgage payments and sheriff's sales, to affect the politics of 1788.

To understand the landlord-tenant struggle, and the conflict of political parties which grew from it, it will help to take a quick overview of land tenure and politics in Dutchess in the seventeen-fifties. The owner or owners of a patent very often did not live on or even visit their land. There is no record of Henry Beekman, Jr., ever setting foot in his Beekman Back Lots, while "the widow Pawling came over from Rhinebeck once a year in a lumberwagon to collect her rents."[6] Patents were often purchased for scandalously small sums. Thus, Lord Bellomont wrote to the secretary of the Board of Trade in 1698:

> One Henry Beekman, a Lieutenant Colonel in the militia, has a vast tract of land as large as the Midling county of England, for which he gave Fletcher [the governor] a hundred dollars, about 25 pounds English, and I am told he values his purchase at £5000.[7]

38

Often the patents were illegal, in that no proper purchase from the Indians was ever made. This was preeminently true of the Philipse Patent, embracing all of southern Dutchess. Professors Mark and Handlin call it "undoubtedly fraudulent," and in the nineteenth century, when it was safe to do so, the New York legislature said the same—adding, however, that to call it in question at that late date "would unsettle the title to a large portion of the State."[8] Moreover, by loosely specifying unsurveyed boundaries, patentees frequently contrived to take possession of many times the acreage intended by the government. Here, too, the Philipse Patent is a prime example. The eastern boundary was a certain "marked tree," which as originally intended would have limited the patent to 15,000 acres; but by asserting that the tree was really somewhere very different, Philipse succeeded in adding 190,000 extra acres to his claim.[9]

Having taken possession, patentees were slow to survey and divide their holdings. In Dutchess it was after 1750 when all the land was made available for actual farming. Whether the patent was leased or sold varied from owner to owner. In Rombout one of the three owners, Catherine Brett, began to sell at once, disposed of 30,000 acres, and in 1760 was rated at only twenty pounds;[10] whereas the Verplanck family, holding another third of that patent, maintained a strict leasehold policy into the nineteenth century. Very generally, north and south Dutchess were predominantly in leasehold until the Revolution, while central Dutchess—the precincts of Rombout, Poughkeepsie, Charlotte, and Amenia—was predominantly in freehold.[11] What the Revolution did was to make south Dutchess, as well as central Dutchess, predominantly freehold (see map on p. 40).

Whereas in older leases the tenant was compelled to render a variety of physical services, the relation between landlord and tenant came increasingly to be expressed in money. A series of leases from 1742 to 1787 in the Gilbert Livingston Land Papers show the transition toward the cash nexus.[12] The earlier leases

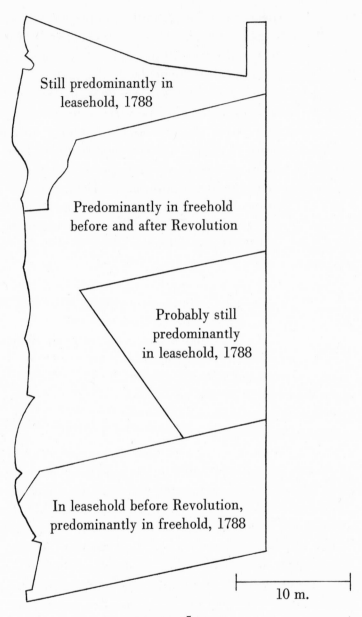

Still predominantly in
leasehold, 1788

Predominantly in freehold
before and after Revolution

Probably still
predominantly
in leasehold, 1788

In leasehold before Revolution,
predominantly in freehold, 1788

10 m.

FIGURE 5

Map of Types of Land Tenure

40

provide for payment in kind (so many bushels of "good sweet merchantable winter wheat"), a "couple of live fat hens," and a day's work with wagon or seven shillings. In a lease of 1758 the same printed form is used but the clauses about the hens and a day's work are crossed out. In a lease of 1767 a new printed form is used which mentions neither fowls nor carting, but still provides for payment in kind. The last in the series, dated 1787, provides for a cash rent. Clauses that remain throughout the series are those providing for reentry or seizure of goods by the landlord in the event of default of rent, those prohibiting waste, especially of timber, and those which require the tenant to grind his grain at the landlord's mill and to offer his grain for sale to the landlord before anyone else. Thus the manorial lease shaded off into the cash lease, as the cash lease was to shade off into mortgage indebtedness.

Given this centralized economic power, politics could be only partially democratic at best. Even had the universal manhood suffrage of the 1788 election existed in the seventeen-fifties, what Namier calls "the inevitable result of open voting by people in dependent positions" would have had its effect.[13] Namier, writing of England in the same period, estimates that only one voter in twenty had sufficient economic and social independence to cast an independent vote.[14] And in fact, of course, voting for the New York Assembly was restricted to owners of forty-pound freeholds. Tenants with lands of this value whose leases ran for more than twenty-one years enjoyed the suffrage, but freeholders with lands worth less than forty pounds did not. The number of eligible voters, therefore, could not have greatly surpassed the number of freeholders, and these were as follows: In 1713-1714, out of a total population of 445, there were 89 adult males and 67 freeholders; in 1740-1746, out of a total population of 8,806, there were 2,056 adult males and 235 freeholders; in 1771-1775, out of a total population of 22,404, there were 4,687 adult males and 1,800 freeholders.[15] The percentage of freeholders to adult white males, then, was 75 percent in 1713-1714, 11 percent in 1740-1746, and 38 percent in 1771-1775. Estimates which credited Dutchess with 2,500 militiamen in the French and Indian War,[16] and 10,000 in the Revolution,[17] would make the last two percentages still lower. In consequence, Milton Klein's recent suggestion that 65 percent of the rural adult male population in colonial New York could vote[18] appears too high for Dutchess County, and Irving Mark's suggested total of 53 percent for six rural counties in 1777[19] appears too high for the colonial period. It would seem safe to say that in colonial Dutchess, as in colonial Virginia,[20] less than half of the adult white males enjoyed the franchise.[21]

The political boss of Dutchess from roughly 1725 to 1758 was its largest landowner, Henry Beekman, Jr. From his perennial seat in the Assembly, Beekman sent home a fascinating series of instructions to his agent on the spot, the clerk of Dutchess County, Henry Livingston.[22] Livingston acted both as Beekman's campaign manager and as his rent collector. A letter from Beekman might run:

> I find let me take what method in getting my rents or debt in meets with so much difficulty. Clement West bought from Jonathan Strickland without my consent to whom I have leased said farm. William Humphrey told me something about West but have forgot what and he is as poor as [name omitted in D.C.H.S., *Yearbook*] and Wiltsie has no lease and is as poor. If you know of no remedy to keep these two actions between hawks and buzzards let them drop . . .[23]

Or again it might say:

> Have writ a long Dutch letter to Mr. Hendrick Kip and sent him the last votes I had with direction to be left at Capt. H. Terboss for perusal of friends there at Judge Ter Boss Du Boys etc. another letter to Judge Boss Benjamin Ferris H. Filkin Will Humphreys Gert Van Wagenen Gert Benthuyse Sister Pawling . . . So have disposed five sets of votes sundry of the council and assembly addresses am tired of writing over and over the same story.[24]

42

Running for office in Dutchess County required what was called in Virginia, "swilling the planters with bumbo."[25] Pursuant to the elections of 1752, Beekman wrote to his campaign manager, Livingston:

> Mr. Filkin said he would provide or furnish beef pork and backing. Most all should be built a day or two before the election and brought to the several houses of ours as Buys, Van de Bogart or Mrs. Ten Brock. Baltus Van Kleek bond he count six barrels of cider I had bespoke of Colonel Van Kleek. The cider should also be distributed before the day. I will send you my Negro Sam till the election be over. Bread we intend to bake here 100 rum are to have from Bowdwyn that also should be distributed to such houses wherein it cannot be had.[26]

Beekman controlled the governor's appointments of sheriff, coroners, militia officers, and justices of the peace for Dutchess County.[27] "So routine were patronage matters to Henry in 1744," White comments, "that he confessed to his nephew and political lieutenant, Henry Livingston, that he had forgotten on a trip home 'to consult for a fit person to be Coroner.' "[28] In 1743 he had written Livingston:

> . . . also, that you send down a list of five commissioners of the peace as it is now circumstanced, and judges and assistants for keeping the courts . . . and who would suit best and convenientest for assistants case of a new commission. I should only surmize as Judge Terboss, Filkin, Swartwout, assistant H. Beekman [himself] Mathew DuBoys, Lou Van Kleek, Cornelius Van Wyck, Gul. Verplank, Henry VanDerburgh.[29]

Then as now, money might grease the machinery of appointment:

> Louis DuBoys of your place told me he would this day apply to the governor for a Captain's license for himself if Doctor Colden be gone home he will perhaps be elsewhere not understood. Money only hath sense.[30]

The practical consequence of an "interest" or "connection" in provincial New York is suggested by the following letter describing Colonel Beekman's influence. In 1753, Joseph Alexander wrote to Joseph Murray:

> There is little probability that impartial jury can be found in that county [Dutchess] to try those causes. For all the first Nine Partners are concerned against us. . . . The greatest part of the rest of the land in the county either Col. Beekman or his sisters or their relations or the owners of the two Nine Partners or their relations are concerned in and the very few men that are unconcerned in that county . . .

He would accept, Alexander concluded, a jury "of any foreign county except Albany and Ulster where Col. Beekman has great interest and relations."[31]

Beekman was occasionally challenged for election by rival landowners who wished to secure some of this valuable patronage, but he held his seat until in 1758 he voluntarily retired.[32] In letters of 1749-1751, however, we hear rumblings of a different kind of discontent. On December 19, 1751, Beekman wrote to Livingston:

> As to the affair of our tenant have had item four or five months ago, kept the thing a secret with intent to find its first mover, then suspecting the person you do hope you'll find out who those were, at the Poughkeepsie meeting truth will come out, and the authors of rebellion, seducers—give them rope enough they will hang themselves. So passiance.[33]

The rebels and seducers referred to were the first movers in the tenant discontent which was to overturn the political machine Beekman built. Centering in the south, the discontent also affected Beekman's eastern holdings in the precincts of Beekman and Pawling. To the story of that discontent we now turn.

Southern Dutchess, in which the tenant riots of 1766 centered, was in many ways separated from the rest of Dutchess County. A high ridge, culminating at the Hudson with Mt. Beacon, Breakneck Ridge, and Anthony's Nose, made north-south travel arduous; even a modern road map shows how the farmers of Patterson and Carmel took their wheat southwest to Cold Springs and Peekskill rather than over "the mountains" to Fishkill (now Beacon). The soil of this southern region was generally poor and rocky. "The south part of the county," wrote William Smith in 1756, "is mountainous and fit only for iron works."[34] Finally, it was only in the seventeen-fifties, later than anywhere else in Dutchess County, that the land of the southern region was surveyed, subdivided, and leased out in farms.[35] Thus, in respect to isolation, poor soil, and late settlement, this was Dutchess County's frontier.

This was the area, as we saw in the last chapter, which voted consistently Clintonian in the seventeen-nineties, when north Dutchess was consistently Federalist and central Dutchess wavered between the two. Although none of the seven Dutchess delegates at the ratifying convention came from the region, two came from precincts just to the north (Swartwout from Rombout, Akin from Pawling), and these were the two who voted against the Constitution when the blue chips were down. Here, it seemed likely, was the heart of the voting power of Dutchess Anti-Federalism, the soil from which sentiments like those of "One of Many" (Chapter 1) sprang.

Such was the stage. The dramatis personnae fell into two camps. On the one hand were the three heirs to the Philipse Patent, which embraced the entire 205,000 acres: Philip Philipse, son of the patentee, and two British army officers, Roger Morris and Beverly Robinson, who married Philipse's two daughters. On the other hand were the settlers, who came almost entirely from New England[36] and numbered just under nine thousand by 1788.[37] They came, in the words of a Moravian missionary, "in expectation of bettering their fortunes by the purchase of cheap farms, and for the enjoyment of religious liberty,"[38] naming their hamlets Carmel, Sharon, and Amenia, as their descendants would found Lebanon and Sweet Home at the end of the Oregon Trail. For most of them it was to be a long day before they could enjoy the fruits of the land under their own vine and fig tree, and be not afraid.

Three types of grievance brought things to a head in southern Dutchess. The first involved all the tenants on the Philipse Patent and was tersely summarized by one of the 1766 rioters as "largeness of rents and shortness of leases."[39] The Philipse heirs followed a rigorous policy of lease rather than sale; down to the Revolution, only one farm on the patent had been sold. Many of the leases ran for only one year and were secured by a penal bond of one thousand pounds. Whereas most Dutchess landlords were nonresident, Morris and Robinson moved onto the land and instituted a close supervision more characteristic of the manors. Robinson's cool, aggressive intelligence set its stamp on all the subsequent events. For example, when on one occasion the tenants contested the validity of the Philipse Patent before a Court of Chancery, Robinson suddenly produced (but did not permit the tenants to see) what purported to be a record of sale by the Indians, and by this "obvious forgery"[40] he managed to carry the day.

The second grievance involved only a few tenants directly, but threatened many more. For decades before 1754, settlers had filtered onto the Philipse Patent. They took leases, when they took them at all, from the only apparent owners, the Wappinger Indians. This tribe claimed ownership of the east bank of the Hudson from Yonkers to Poughkeepsie, but by mid-century had retreated to the most inhospitable fragment of this area, the southern Dutchess highlands. At the outbreak of the French and Indian War the men of the tribe left to fight for the British, leaving their women and children at the Indian settlement in Stockbridge, Massachusetts. On their return to the highlands they found the Philipse heirs in possession, and commenced a legal action which they carried to the New York Supreme Court, to the governor and his council sitting as a Court of Chancery, and to the lords of trade in England.[41]

46

In this legal action the Indians were allied with the white squatters on the Philipse Patent. Fifteen of these squatters, some of whom had farmed the land for thirty or forty years, Robinson attempted to eject, without, as the tenants said,

> any manner of recompense for their labour, fatigue, and expense in cultivating manuring clearing fencing and improving said lands, nor for their buildings thereon erected, nor for their crops thereon then growing.[42]

"Being chiefly poor people," the tenants explained, they "unitedly agreed to stand trial in only one" of the fifteen cases of ejectment; but they "found that every attorney at law in that whole province was previously retained on the other side."[43] The Indians thereupon had a tenant, Samuel Munroe, acknowledged as their attorney by two justices of the peace, and proceeded with their case. As their suit was rejected and roughly rebuked by courts entirely made up of large-scale landowners and land speculators, they and their neighbors cast about for some other means of redress.[44]

Since in the course of this chronicle we shall rarely have the opportunity of listening to the tenants themselves express their discontents, it may not be amiss to quote at some length from petitions of the tenants preserved among Samuel Munroe's papers at the New York Historical Society. One of these, dated November 10, 1763, and entitled, "A petition for a Confirmation of our inheritance together with our associates," describes the contested area between the Rombout and Philipse patents and states:

> This land has been claimed by both Philipse and Col. Beekman which has discouraged people from building good houses etc. and planting orchards and some have been disinherited and the given leases of Col. Beekman are intolerable.

Another petition, of February 24, 1764, says, again in a long sentence which seems to express the bursting out of grievances all in one breath:

We the subjects abovesaid finding possessions and livings on a tract of vacant land and unpatented or not granted to any by the King's letters patent though claimed by several and the civil inhabitants put to great damage and difficulty being disinherited and thrown out of possession at the same time the Claimers refusing to give their obedient tenants a good or warrantable title by leases deed or any other title for their leases for 3 lives or twenty years: theirs only to quit their claims their resolution especially Capt. R...n...ns in November intolerable for he would not lease the land to the inhabitants who had lived on it for near 30 years past and had manured and cultivated the same but would oblige them to buy their farms paying money down for it or else to remove immediately . . .

Samuel Munroe was a principal sufferer from the third type of grievance which agitated the tenants of south Dutchess. Because of the vagueness of patent boundaries, there was a disputed strip or "gore" between almost every pair of adjoining patents. Litigation usually ended in compromise, and the ejectment of tenants unlucky enough to live on the wrong side of the compromise line. Indeed, the standard method of settling a boundary was to eject a tenant and go to court. When the rival patents lay in different states, as they did along New York's eastern boundary, litigation often gave way to armed conflict.

The Philipse heirs were late in the field and quickly became embroiled with the owners of the Rombout and Beekman patents to the north, and with a Connecticut group of patentees who claimed land in the Oblong (see diagram). Samuel Munroe held land both in the disputed Beekman gore and (either at the same time or later) under a Connecticut lease in the Oblong; so did the family of the Jonathan Akin who was to vote against the Constitution at Poughkeepsie in 1788.[45] This convergence of two boundary disputes in the neighborhood of Quaker Hill and Patterson was what made it the center of the tenant rising. When on March 11, 1766, arbitrators upheld the Robinson rather than the Connecticut claim to the Oblong lands,[46] the dry tinder of cumulative grievance burst into flame.

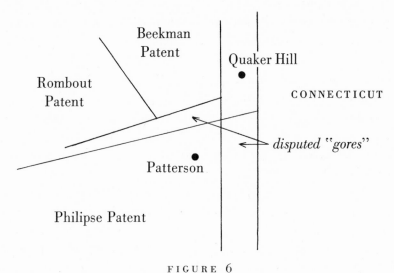

FIGURE 6

Map of Site of Tenant Rebellion, 1766

During the winter, in the after-harvest talk at Morrison's and Towner's taverns,[47] a plan of action had crystallized and now was put into effect. When May came no rents were paid. Tenants who attempted to make an individual settlement were visited at night by groups of their neighbors armed with clubs and rifles. William Prendergast, a well-respected man rather more prosperous than most of his following,[48] was induced to become the tenants' leader. A committee of twelve was set up to assist him, militia companies were formed, and captains elected. Local justices of the peace were forbidden to serve judicial process on days when the tenants were meeting; the tenants undertook to rescue any of their number who should be imprisoned.

This was essentially a waiting game, more like a strike than a *jacquerie*. Much time was lost in parading up and down the countryside under arms, in forcing justices to swear never to prosecute the rebels. Two kinds of direct action, however, were initiated. Armed mobs visited the homes where men had been

ejected, dispossessed the new tenants put in by Robinson, and
restored the original occupants. When one of their comrades,
John Way, was imprisoned in Poughkeepsie, the tenants turned
up in force, overawed the sheriff and justices, and took Way
home with them. This was on June 6. The next men captured by
the authorities were jailed in New York City. The tenants then
marched on the city, confidently expecting welcome and assistance from the metropolitan Sons of Liberty. When this failed to
materialize, they hesitated on the outskirts of the city and finally
went back home.

No doubt it was this abortive gesture which spurred the
sending of British troops. After it was realized that the Dutchess
militia was undependable and that at least two thousand tenants
were up in arms,[49] regiments of British soldiers with cannon
were landed at Poughkeepsie and marched on Quaker Hill. As
they marched east past the homes of rebellious tenants, the
soldiers "burnt and destroyed some of their houses, pillaged and
plundered others, stove in their cider barrels, turned their provisions out . . . into the open streets, ripped open their feather
beds."[50] There had been brave talk in May and June that mobs
had dealt with kings before this, and that if redcoats were sent
they would meet muskets behind every hedge and bush. But
the time for Lexington and Concord was not yet. After a few
skirmishes in which one British soldier was mortally wounded,
the tenants surrendered.

In sixty trials in July and August, tenants received sentences
of varying severity, and Prendergast was condemned to death
for high treason. One of his judges recalled ten years later that
when sentence on Prendergast was pronounced, "the prisoner
fell like a slaughtered ox, the commissioners hung down their
heads and sighs and groans arose from every corner of the
house."[51] James Livingston, Dutchess sheriff, advertised in the
papers for men to assist in the execution, guaranteeing anonym-
ity. No one volunteered, and it may have been this which saved

Prendergast's life; for his wife, Mehitabel Wing, galloped to New York City and received a stay from Governor Moore pending an appeal to the king, which was ultimately successful.

This tragicomic ending should not blind us to the lasting significance of the tenants' rebellion. Men had been forced to take sides and the choices they made were not soon forgotten. It was not only Secretary Conway and Governor Moore who spoke of the rioters as "the lower and more ignorant of the people," "the lowest people." [52] John Morin Scott, the Son of Liberty, was a member of the Supreme Court which mocked Munroe and Nimham (the Wappinger chieftan).[53] The sheriff who attempted to rally the Dutchess militia against the tenants was James Livingston, a ne'er-do-well uncle of Gilbert Livingston; the sheriff of Albany County who led troops against Livingston Manor rioters was a Yates. The jury which condemned Prendergast was composed of some of the very men who would later make political capital from the tenant grievances: two Brinckerhoffs, related to the assemblyman elected by tenant votes in 1768; Jacob Griffin, political crony and near neighbor of Dirck Brinckerhoff and Jacobus Swartwout.[54] In the pattern of reactions to the crisis of 1766 was anticipated the future division between radicals and conservatives in the Revolution, between Anti-Federalists and Federalists, and between more and less ardent Anti-Federalists in 1788.

The immediate result of the political moment of truth in 1766 was the startling outcome of the 1768 elections. Henry Beekman, on his political retirement, had arranged that Dutchess be represented in the Assembly by his old lieutenant, Henry Livingston of Poughkeepsie, and by Robert R. Livingston of Clermont, the father of Chancellor Livingston. They held the seats from 1761 to 1768 but were defeated in 1768 by Leonard Van Kleek and Dirck Brinckerhoff, although Livingston, as Cadwallader Colden reported to his superiors in England, "had everything in his favour, which power could give him."[55]

The meaning of the election was twofold. Van Kleek and Brinckerhoff were far from being poor tenants. Van Kleek paid more taxes than anyone in Poughkeepsie,[56] while Brinckerhoff was affluent enough to lend £7,664 in mortgages between 1768 and 1785.[57] They represented, in White's words, "a rising middle class of freeholders which disliked the domination of the landed aristocracy,"[58] the class which consistently supplied the political leadership of Dutchess Anti-Federalism. Beekman had made a fatal mistake in choosing two candidates from the same family. No doubt the fact that Robert Livingston was his son-in-law blinded him to the political liabilities of an aristocrat, a nonresident, and a second Livingston. Namier says that in England it was usual to nominate one aristocrat and one county gentleman: "hardly ever was an attempt made in a county to fill both seats with members of the same family," for fear of alienating the middling county gentry.[59]

Van Kleek and Brinckerhoff were elected partly by the votes of tenants, some of whom were from that part of the county which two years before had been raising more hell than wheat. We know this from two sources. One is the statement of Robert C. Livingston that his kinsman had been beaten by the votes of the tenants of Beekman and Robert G. Livingston, whose lands were in the precinct of Beekman in southeast Dutchess.[60] The other is the following poem written by a twelve-year-old boy, William Moore, Jr., of Oswego, Beekman Precinct:

> One night in my slumbers, I saw in a dream
> Judge Livingston's party contriving a scheme
> To set up great papers and give some great bounty
> For to be assemblymen in Dutchess County.
> But Leonard [Van Kleek] and Derrick [Brinckerhoff] are
>   both chosen men,
> The Livingstons won't get a vote to their ten,
> So pull down your papers, talk no more of bounty,
> You can't be assemblymen in Dutchess County.
>   Your printed relation

> Wants confirmation
> Tho' signed by Judge Thomas' hand
>   Your writings are discreet
>   But in them there's deceit
> Not a vote would you get if it wan't for your land.[61]

Defeated in the election, the conservative party had recourse to the governor's control of appointments. The key officials in county administration were the sheriff and chief judge. In 1769 and 1771, Dutchess received new men in each of these posts. The sheriff was Philip J. Livingston, of Livingston Manor; the chief judge was Beverly Robinson.[62] They held their posts until the Revolutionary broom swept all clean.[63]

Thus from 1768 to 1776 an uneasy truce prevailed in Dutchess County. Judges were one thing, juries another. Gilbert Livingston wrote to Robert G. Livingston in 1773:

> On mature consideration I think it much the best not to commence a suit against him here in the county court, as he is one of the assistant justices himself, and it will be tried by a jury who will be perhaps half of them in the mob interest.[64]

Beverly Robinson wrote to his lawyer, James Duane, just after the riots were suppressed: "I dare say that you do imagine after the correction that our rioters have lately had I should enjoy my lands in peace and quietness, but it seems my troubles are not yet at an end."[65] In 1773, with the legal help of Duane, Scott, and Bartholomew Crannell (Gilbert Livingston's father-in-law), Robinson was still trying to "eject old Samuel Munroe."[66]

In 1777, John Watts, a Dutchess landowner and a member of the Supreme Court in 1766, wrote that "the counties of Albany, Dutchess and Westchester, in the province of New York, are in an absolute state of vassalage, being all tenants at will to Rensalear, Livingston, Beekman and Philipse"; a promise to make them freeholders "would instantly bring you at least six thousand able farmers into the field."[67] In Dutchess, British agents were already acting on Watts' advice. In December 1775,

Samuel Dodge (a future commissioner of forfeitures) wrote to the president of the Provincial Congress:

> There are several very officious Ministerial agents in the county, who have corrupted the minds of many of the ignorant and baser sort of men among us, maliciously telling them the Whigs were in rebellion; the King would conquer them, and their estates be forfeited; and if they take up arms against them, the King for their services will give them the Whigs' possessions.[68]

THE SALE OF LOYALIST LANDS,

1780-1785:

THE PARTY CONFLICT RENEWED

The tenants here are great villains. Some of them are
resolved to take advantage of the times and make their landlords
give them leases forever.
Henry Livingston to Robert R. Livingston, 1775

May He give us peace and independence and deliverance from
the persecutions of the lower class who I foresee will be
as despotic as any prince (if not more so) in Europe.
Margaret Beekman Livingston to Robert R. Livingston, 1779

In an effort to determine how much reality underlay the
class-conscious party propaganda of 1788, the preceding chapters examined, first, the leading personnel of the Dutchess Federalists and Anti-Federalists, and second, the creation in the
seventeen-sixties of a political party or grouping to oppose the
traditional dominance of the largest landed families. The present chapter examines the impact of the Revolution on this prewar
political alignment. It shows how the county's radical and conservative political tendencies at first joined hands in common
support of the war with England, but how, by 1779, the coalition
had begun to split into its pre-Revolutionary wings over the issue

55

of sequestration and sale of Loyalist lands. The issue of the Loyalist lands is the connecting link between Dutchess politics before and after the Revolution. It is the proof that in this county the concept of two-party continuity, far from being "mossy," is the only possible way to understand the politics of the Revolutionary era.

Looking back, it is easy to underestimate the meaning of the bill to sell Loyalist estates. No doubt the bill merely accelerated a long-run trend toward freehold tenure which, bill or no bill, would have triumphed in the end. As earlier noted, the percentage of freeholders in the adult male population of Dutchess County doubled in the generation between 1745 and the Revolution. Hard-bitten landlords like Robert G. Livingston still sold off a farm here, a farm there, finding it more convenient to hold mortgages on freeholds than to try to control a tenant's management of the land.[1] In a continental economy with much land and few hands to work it, the neofeudal land system of the Hudson Valley could not have long survived. Quite apart from the Revolution, the flood of New England immigrants and the Yankee egalitarianism they brought with them would have swept it away —as McCracken observes, all the leaders of the pre-Revolutionary tenant riots were New Englanders.[2]

So it seems looking back. But to contemporaries, living through the event and making it, the law would seem to have had a more comprehensive symbolic significance. It was the first major breakthrough of the political revolution into social change; with this dike gone, who could tell how far the waters would spread? Only this fear can explain why in Dutchess County, as in the state as a whole, the struggle for the bill became a political watershed. "Thereafter," Allan Nevins writes, "the patriots were clearly divided into moderate and extremist factions . . ."[3] And Spaulding confirms: "The Confiscation Act for the first time aroused a conservative Whig opposition to the extreme measures of the government."[4]

56

Even in the first days of the Revolution, the unity of Dutchess Whigs was not altogether cordial. Early in April 1775, a meeting of persons from the precincts of Rhinebeck, Northeast, Amenia, and Rombout "elected" as delegates to the First Provincial Congress Egbert Benson, Morris Graham, and Robert R. Livingston, Jr.[5] A letter to the *New York Packet* hotly protested that Charlotte had voted 140-35 against sending delegates, Poughkeepsie 110-77, and that the eastern and southeastern precincts of Beekman, Pawling, Southeast, Fredericksburgh, and Philipse were "almost unanimously opposed." These seven precincts were said to contain three fourths of the county population.[6] As for the three delegates, Benson was the future leader of Dutchess Federalism, Graham was a large landlord in the northeastern part of the county, and Livingston was the chancellor-to-be already several times encountered.

In reply, another anonymous letter writer stated that the 1,800 freeholders of Dutchess were two to one in favor of sending these delegates, and challenged the first writer to produce a list of signatures.[7] The latter, writing after the news of Lexington and Concord reached New York, was unexpectedly conciliatory: He did not wish to pursue the argument, for "a coalition of parties in the County of *Dutchess* will probably very soon take place."[8] It was, in fact, the next day that a new ten-man delegation was chosen. It hardly represented a "coalition." Benson, Graham, and Livingston were excluded and replaced by a group including Melancton Smith, Ephraim Paine, Dirck Brinckerhoff, Gilbert Livingston, and Zephaniah Platt: the principal leaders of the Dutchess popular party down to 1788.[9]

The manner of electing these delegates was a revolution in itself. It was "the freeholders and inhabitants" of Poughkeepsie, the "inhabitants of Charlotte Precinct" who made these decisions; it was the "freemen, freeholders and inhabitants" of the county who were asked to sign the Association in support of the Provincial Congress.[10] The secret ballot was not yet; the election

57

of May 1775 was by "a majority of voices," and a move to have delegates to the next Provincial Congress elected by secret ballot was defeated.[11] But it was universal manhood suffrage. The attempt to write this into the constitution of 1777 failed,[12] and the property qualification was not waived again until the election of 1788, nor in the regular elections of New York until the eighteen-twenties.

The Dutchess delegations to the Second and Third Provincial congresses, and to the Provincial Convention, showed a conservative trend. Morris Graham was back in the second and third congresses; Robert R. Livingston in the third congress and in the Provincial Convention; Egbert Benson became chairman of the County Committee of Safety. Included also were some of the most aggressive landlords—Beverly Robinson in the second congress, Robert G. Livingston in the same, and Sheriff James Livingston of 1766 notoriety in the third congress and the Provincial Convention.[13] Moreover, at this time even the popular leaders lagged behind rank-and-file sentiment. In June 1777, Zephaniah Platt, Christopher Tappen, and Charles DeWitt joined John Jay and Mathew Cantine in urging the nomination of Philip Schuyler as governor and George Clinton as lieutenant governor. They wrote Clinton that committees from Orange, Ulster, and Dutchess would meet on June 3 to nominate men for the "great offices of government." The significant postscript is added: "P.S. Unless the sentiments of the majority should be very obvious, avoid binding yourself to abide their determination."[14]

The Schuyler-Clinton slate, presumably representing the "coalition of parties" mentioned above, was rejected by the voters, who gave Clinton the largest number of votes for both offices.[15] To the consternation of many, not least of Schuyler himself, the popular party took over the state government.

As the war dragged on, future Federalists and Anti-Federalists labored together on dozens of overlapping Revolutionary committees in Dutchess. Striving to cope with an endless series

58

of administrative emergencies, they increasingly found themselves attacked from behind, as it were, by a rising popular discontent. The discontent centered in three areas: the militia, the
cost of living, and the land.

From the beginning, conservative Whigs had seen in the
militia a threat to their control. James Duane wrote to Robert R.
Livingston in 1775:

> I am much pleased that young Mr. Livingston is raising a company
> in the Manor. I wish he may extend his views further, in the only
> plan, which, independent of the grand contest, will render landed
> property secure. We must think in time of the means of assuring
> the reins of government when these commotions shall subside. Li-
> centiousness is the natural object of civil ["war" crossed out by
> Duane in the manuscript] discord and it can only be guarded
> against by placing the command of the troops in the hands of men
> of property and rank who, by that means, will preserve the same
> authority over the minds of the people which they enjoyed in the
> time of tranquility.[16]

But the men of property and rank did not control the militia in
Dutchess. The three large landlords of south Dutchess—Philipse,
Morris, and Robinson—were all Loyalists. It is true that the
well-to-do Morris Graham and Richard D'Cantillon were lieutenant colonel and major, respectively. But Dirck Brinckerhoff, the
popular assemblyman elected in 1768, was also a colonel; and
Brinckerhoff's friend Jacobus Swartwout,[17] one of the two Dutchess delegates to vote against the Constitution in 1788, rose from
colonel to general to be the highest-ranking officer in the county.
These higher officers were appointed at a county or state level.
From the rank of captain down, militia officers were elected by
the common soldiers. In Dutchess the lower officers so chosen
were a mixed bag of future Federalists and Anti-Federalists,
many of whom by virtue of their popularity would represent
Dutchess in the Assembly in the seventeen-eighties.[18]

If the officers were uncertain, the men were much more so.
Egbert Benson wrote to the Provincial Convention on July 15,

1776, that of the four hundred militiamen in Rhinebeck, one hundred had been disarmed for suspected disloyalty, and he doubted whether there were two precincts in the county with less disaffection.[19] The reason for the soldiers' dissatisfaction is not far to seek. A militia colonel received seventy-five dollars a month, a private six dollars and sixty-six cents.[20] In August 1776, Zephaniah Platt wrote to the Provincial Convention that "there is great complaints amongst the troops concerning this bounty, many of them having no money to purchase necessaries, having left at home what little they had for the use of their families."[21] George Clinton wrote to the Continental Committee of Safety a year later:

> The continental pay and rations being far below the wages given for ordinary labor the difference becomes a tax rendered by personal service and as the train band list (from the exemptions arising from age, office and other causes) consists chiefly of the middling and lower class of people, this extraordinary tax is altogether paid by them.[22]

The extraordinary tax bore with particular severity on the poor tenant militiamen of south Dutchess. In this area every militia officer was a tenant.[23] Their colonel, Luddington, wrote to George Clinton on May 1, 1781:

> At best the regiment are very poor when compared with other regiments and are called on to raise an equal number with the others, when I can affirm that ten farmers in Col. Brinckerhoff's regiment is able to purchase the whole of mine. In this unequal way, I have been obliged to turn out of my men until they are so much impoverished that they almost despair.[24]

This was written in 1781. But as early as the spring of 1777, the three commissioners for detecting conspiracies, Swartwout, Benson, and Smith, were

> laboring to enforce discipline among mutinous and rebellious members of the militia, especially in Colonel John Freer's regiment which was the Poughkeepsie Regiment and in Colonel Henry Luddington's

regiment in the southeastern part of the county. Much of the trouble was doubtless due to the failure on the part of the militia members to receive the bounty due them from the State.[25]

In the same spring, special three-man commissions visited the most heavily tenanted areas, Livingston Manor in the north and Philipse Patent in the south, to search out disloyalty. On May 8, Zephaniah Platt, Mathew Cantine, and Robert R. Livingston reported to the Provincial Convention of the State of New York that on the Livingston Manor almost everyone was disaffected, especially in the eastern part.[26]

This is a side of the Revolution too often forgotten. If for government contractors like Melancton Smith and Mathew Patterson the Revolution meant one swift bound from obscurity to riches, for thousands of common soldiers it meant permanent impoverishment.

> Many who served in the ranks were industrious men who had acquired a little foothold in life and owned small farms. The colonists were straightened for means wherewith to carry on the war, and pay for the soldiers was uncertain and slow in arriving. Some served for years without being able to draw their small pay, and meantime their families at home were getting deeper and deeper in debt for their necessary subsistence.
>
> When the war ended and they at last received their pay it was in continental currency which at once became worthless. By this means the men who had done patient duty in the army for years returned home only to lose their farms and homesteads, and discouraged by their losses and by the general confusion in political and industrial affairs, many lost hope and courage and drifted into vagrancy.

"My mother," continues the writer, an Amenia resident,

> was born in 1800, and she often recalled that during her early life there were many tramps of a certain type travelling the country roads. . . . Rarely or never were their requests for food, drink, or lodging denied, for it was well known that they were old Revolutionary soldiers impoverished in the wars.[27]

The distress of Dutchess militiamen is suggested by the frequent advertisements for the apprehension of deserters which appeared

61

in the *New York Journal* and *New York Packet* (New York City newspapers published during the Revolution in Poughkeepsie and Fishkill, respectively).

In these newspapers one finds also the story of the second great popular grievance in Revolutionary Dutchess: speculation in foodstuffs and the high cost of living. As early as December 1776, Henry Luddington and others wrote to the Council of Safety inveighing against the

> wicked, mercenary intrigues of a number of ingrossing jockies, who have drained this part of the State of the article of bread to that degree, that we have reason to fear there is not enough left for the support of the inhabitants.[28]

Discontent on this head became acute in the year 1779, during which the continental currency depreciated from something like one eighth the value of specie to perhaps one fortieth. The resulting price rise is suggested by figures in the Papers of the Commissioners for Sequestration—Dutchess County, at the New York Historical Society: A Negro slave girl sold for £50 on December 23, 1777, and for £3,680 on October 5, 1780; on August 16, 1780, a pair of oxen was sold for £1,040.

Throughout America the public expressed its indignation at the rising cost of living by reviving the local committees of the first days of the Revolution.[29] The rationale of these committees was the belief that monopolistic practices of merchants and dishonesty of public officials were causing the price rise. The committeemen reasoned that if local scrutiny and extralegal direct action could be brought to bear, inflation might be checked. "At length," wrote a correspondent to the *New York Packet* on July 15, 1779,

> is the virtuous part of the community alarmed, and the old and true friends to their country again step forth to remedy evils the laws cannot reach, by the exertion of Committees, the terror of all villains. . . . Let no time be lost then, my countrymen, in forming your Committees. . . . As soon as the authority of your Committees ended,

Knavery shewed its head, villains of every class came forth and practiced with impunity.

This fascinating process of self-organization can only be glanced at here, as the prelude to the movement for confiscating Loyalist lands. The Dutchess committees were inspired by the example of Philadelphia, whose price-fixing committee called in July 1779 for the formation of committees "in every State and county."[30] Within a week, Rombout Precinct had set up a committee with the future Anti-Federalist Jacobus Swartwout as chairman.[31] This committee announced that traders were to buy goods only at prices fixed by the committee and sell them only at designated rates of profit, after invoices had been exhibited to the committee or its chairman.[32] Early in August a committee was formed in Poughkeepsie Precinct, the chairman being future Anti-Federalist Gilbert Livingston.[33] On August 14, Petrus De-Witt, father of future Anti-Federalist John DeWitt, acted as the chairman of a county-wide meeting which resolved to "dilligently inquire into the conduct of all public officers."[34]

Thus, of the three chairmen of these committees whose names are known, two were Anti-Federalist delegates to the ratifying convention of 1788 and the other was the father of a third delegate. Clearly, the leadership of the price-fixing movement of 1779-1780 and of the opposition to the Constitution were substantially the same.

In the same issues of the 1779 papers which told of price-fixing committees starting up in Philadelphia, Boston, and Williamsburg, Dutchess farmers read of the confiscation of Loyalist estates in Pennsylvania, New Jersey, and Vermont.[35] Early in the year there appeared an exchange of letters as to why the estate of Dutchess Tory Thomas Lewis had not been sold.[36] Then in May a correspondent signing himself "Country Man" made an impassioned preelection appeal which underlined the political significance of the confiscation issue. Many other states, he noted, had passed confiscation acts.

It is a matter of the highest regret to great numbers, I might say to the people in general of this State, that similar proceedings have not taken place here, particularly that the confiscation bill was not passed into a law, the last session of Assembly. The public are impatient to know through whose means the completion of that most necessary and important bill was obstructed and put off, tho' they hope it will be one of the first works of the next session. We are also uneasy that the votes of the Legislature are not published, at least in time for us to know before every new election, by the votes of the old one, in what manner they have acquitted themselves, and how well they are entitled to our future choice, which surely no one can have the least pretension to who voted against the confiscation bill.[37]

The movements for price-fixing and for confiscation had a natural relation, for confiscation was widely regarded as an alternative to printing still more currency. In August the Poughkeepsie Precinct price-fixing committee called "for the immediate confiscation and sale of forfeited estates."[38] October 1779, when the New York legislature enacted the permanent confiscation (though not yet the immediate sale) of Loyalist estates, was also the month when national resentment against profiteering reached a climax with the "attack on Fort Wilson" in Philadelphia. The New York Assembly of early 1780, which finally did pass legislation for the sale of confiscated estates, had been specially convened by Governor Clinton for the purpose of dealing with price-fixing proposals.

If Whigs throughout the country saw in Loyalist property a potential prop to Revolutionary finance, the tenants of south Dutchess had additional reasons for wanting the confiscation and sale of Loyalist lands. All of south Dutchess belonged to Loyalist landlords and so might, if confiscated and sold, come into the hands of tenants. Moreover, the influx of patriot refugees from southern New York threatened in 1776-1779 to deprive the long-suffering tenants of even the leaseholds they had.

The much-troubled highlands were the southern boundary of the area controlled by the New York Revolutionary government. Fishkill became a major supply depot for the Army; it was to Fishkill that, after the Battle of White Plains, the corpses were brought back to be stacked like cordwood in the streets. John Jay was only the most prominent of the refugees from West-chester and other southern counties who streamed into the high-lands, often with little more than the clothes on their backs. One of these refugees, John Campbell, wrote to a Dutchess commis-sioner of sequestration in 1780:

> . . . those two families have twelve children the oldest not eleven years old and to my knowledge one of those families have been six weeks this winter without bread—and when the small remains is gone I brought out of New York this must be my situation unless you relieve me.[39]

The departure of Tories as well as the influx of refugees added to the pressure for public management of Loyalist prop-erty. "Almost in every quarter of the county," Egbert Benson and Melancton Smith wrote the president of the New York con-vention in March 1777, "the estates of persons now with the enemy, are daily sold and wasted without any method taken to secure them, either for the public or their creditors."[40]

In that same month the Provincial Convention sought to deal with this problem by creating commissioners of sequestration for each county.[41] The commissioners were empowered, first, to sell the personal effects of Loyalists at public auction, and sec-ond, to lease the lands of Loyalists "under moderate rent from year to year to persons friendly to the cause of America," giving first priority to refugees. Their discharge of the first task does not concern us here.[42] In the second area, the commissioners felt their way into a far more difficult task. In some Loyalist families the head of the house had fled, leaving his wife and children on the farm; should they then be dispossessed?[43] The commissioners had no clear instructions as to how much rent to charge.[44] They were uncertain whether they could lease farms, perhaps belong-ing to an absentee Whig landlord, from which a Tory tenant had

65

departed.[45] On the one hand, they faced protests from men who had left but later returned; Thomas Lewis, whose case was mentioned earlier, wrote to say he had read in the newspaper that his property was to be sold and that justice had certainly miscarried, inscribing his letter, "Poughkeepsie Gaol, Dec. 16, 1778."[46] On the other hand, a precinct committee of safety might remonstrate that the most deserving candidates had been passed over by the commissioners:

> Whereas it is reported that you have let to Mr. John Vredenburgh the farm whereon John Karl formerly lived who is gone off to the enemy, and is now in possession of Lieutenant Furness Knickerbocker; as the right of soil belongs to Mr. Peter Van Benthuysen, the committee of said precinct is not clear whether said place is let by you or Mr. Benthuysen, however that be, said committee beg leave to inform you that Mr. Vredenburgh is not a friend to the cause of America, he only pretends to be neuter, and has already a good house which he occupies, and does not want the other place, unless it be to make gains by, and Lieutenant Knickerbocker . . . has no other place for himself and family than the place which the said Karl left, wherefore this committee recommend Lieutenant Knickerbocker to your justice and favor, and it is the sense of this committee he ought of right to have the preference of said place of which he now is in possession.[47]

In pursuing their difficult assignment, Commissioners Sheldon, Van Wyck, and Livingston stepped into the shoes of the former landlords. They gave leases, with the usual clause forbidding waste.[48] They dispossessed squatters[49] and prosecuted for nonpayment of rent.[50] Since the law stipulated one-year leases, their tenants had each year to seek anew a continuation of leases. Wilhelmys P. [last name illegible] wrote to the commissioners, December 21, 1779:

> As the time I agreed for the place whereon I now live will expire in a few months I take this early opportunity to know whether I can have it for another year and should be glad you would let me know it soon, that I may have time to look elsewhere in case I cannot stay where I now am.[51]

A glimpse of daily life on a farm leased from the commissioners of sequestration is afforded by the account book of the New York City refugee, Jonathan Lawrence.[52] Lawrence "hired" the farm of Daniel Attwater from the commissioners for the year May 1779 to May 1780 (in Dutchess County, elections, town meetings, and the payment of rent took place in the spring). One fourth of the farm Lawrence sublet to his nephew John. In the first spring he planted seventeen bushels of corn, seven bushels of potatoes, and two-and-a-half bushels of buckwheat; the expenses included "1 gallon rum for our plowing frolic." During the summer he paid sums of fifty and thirty-three dollars to soldiers for hoeing his corn and working on his hay. On October 16 he put in the main Dutchess crop, sixteen bushels of wheat. Meantime he pastured "4 Continental Horses" two weeks for the commissary of hospitals. Next spring he changed his crops to flax, rye, and oats. Taxes for the year were sixty-six pounds, rent was sixteen pounds.

The commissioners appear from their records to have attempted to prevent speculators from abusing a law designed to aid refugees. Had they been paragons of justice, however, they could not have easily avoided the charge of favoritism. Leases, unlike the personal effects of Loyalists, were disposed of not at auction but through private application. Often a would-be tenant asked a member of the Revolutionary committee in his neighborhood to write the commissioners on his behalf. A letter from Hugh Rea, chairman of the Northeast Precinct committee, to Commissioner Sheldon, illustrates the difference between the methods of disposal of the two kinds of property. Rea inclosed the inventory of "the personal estates of those that has absconded to the enemy last summer out of this precinct." He urged that they be sold as soon as possible. He said that he could put the movables except the livestock in one safe place, but could not bring together the livestock, as forage was scarce and no one was willing to pasture all the cattle. Rea concluded that the bearer of the letter wished "to hire John Peter Rows place of you, and I would be glad you would assist him in getting it by speaking to the rest of the Commissioners for him."[53]

But the unfairness of the leasing system was more than a matter of favoritism in renting vacant farms. In some cases the commissioners dispossessed an existing tenant to make room for a refugee. How many tenants, one wonders, received letters like the following?

> Messrs. John and Thomas Campbell, Thomas Oakly and Elvin Valentine, refugees from the enemy, have made application to us for the mills, and houses and farm appertaining to the same, and as we are particularly instructed to give refugees the preference we have given those gentlemen our promise, that they may possess the aforementioned premises this present year.
>
> These are therefore to give you notice, that you are to remove.[54]

To James Cox, who received the commissioner's letter, the spirit of '76 may have suddenly seemed less important, and the spirit of '66 more real.

Low militia pay and frequent militia duty, high prices, the example of land sequestration in other states, and the threat of dispossession by refugees[55] put the long-suffering tenants in an ugly mood; nonpayment of rent was widespread.[56] By October 1778, "the respectful address and petition of the freeholders and others, inhabitants of the county of Dutchess," signed by 448 persons, pleaded with the Assembly to speed passage of a bill for selling rather than leasing the forfeited Loyalist lands:

> The delay of this act to another session is big with uncertainty of its passing at all, and therefore of the most dangerous consequences to this State. Especially as it will occasion universal uneasiness and in all probability produce tumults and insurrections, and tend to a domestic tyranny and confusion as much to be dreaded as the evils brought upon us by our connections with Great Britain.[57]

For the tenants, what was at stake was the creation of a policy which seemed to hold out the hope of the freeholds they had

68

fought for and failed to win twelve years before. Simon Calkins and other south Dutchess tenants whom Beverly Robinson had dispossessed in the seventeen-sixties petitioned the legislature on September 2, 1779. They had, they said,

> settled a wild uncultivated tract of land . . . and turned it into comfortable habitations [with an] expectation of reaping the benefit, and enjoying [the fruits of] their labor and toil in the decline of life; being [confident] . . . that whoever should be the proper owner . . . would have justice goodness and compassion . . . to allow them the privilege of enjoying those habitations [and] farms which they had made comfortable and in some measure profitable by the sweat of their brows, upon their paying an equitable and reasonable rent. But contrary to this . . . as soon as their farms were in any measure made comfortable convenient or profitable by their industry, one Beverly Robinson instigated by his associates Philip Philipse and Roger Morris, and assisted by a banditti of King's troops . . . in the year 1776 . . . obliged them to quit their houses and farms and commit themselves naked unto providence.

Therefore, this charred and barely legible document concludes, they desired legislature to "enact such laws or adopt measures as may effect the restoration of these your petitioners."[58]

For the leaders of the popular party in Dutchess, who were to shepherd confiscation legislation through the Assembly, what was at stake was the conversion of sentiments toward violence into votes for reform. One can appreciate the relief with which Commissioner Livingston wrote to Commissioner Van Wyck on March 31, 1780, that the bill had become law. There would be no more leases, Livingston wrote, "as it possibly or rather probably might interfere in the intended sales . . . This regulation will shorten our business beyond the mountain."[59]

Dutchess County sent to the Assembly of 1779-1780, which passed this law, Egbert Benson, Dirck Brinckerhoff, Ananias Cooper, Stephen Dodge, Henry Luddington, Brinton Paine, and Nathaniel Sackett. Benson, Brinckerhoff, and Luddington are familiar faces by now. Dodge was to be one of the new trio of commissioners appointed to sell the Loyalist lands; Paine was a relative of Ephraim Paine, the Revolutionary first judge; Sackett was the man who brought the news of Lexington and Concord to Dutchess County. Two things emerge from the pattern of their votes on the bill to sell Loyalist lands. First, although Luddington was a Federalist-to-be, like Brinckerhoff and Sackett he was from south Dutchess; this may explain why he favored the bill, for it was here that insurrection threatened and here that most of the sales would occur. Second, in the conflict of the delegation's leading figures, Benson and Brinckerhoff, the continuity of the landlord-tenant conflict from 1766 to 1788 is expressed. The one would be Dutchess Federalist leader in 1788, the other was elected by tenant votes after the rising of 1766.

In the legislative session of early 1779, a bill to confiscate the estates of designated Tories had passed the Assembly but failed in the Senate. Robert Livingston wrote to John Jay:

> They have passed a most ill-judged confiscation bill with 200 names in it and so contrived as to give satisfaction to neither party. The Senate are nearly divided about it and have made some amendments which will probably endanger the bill.[60]

This confiscation bill passed in October at the fall session. The struggle then shifted—as incidentally it also shifted in the English and French revolutions (the amount of confiscated land actually sold in France has been estimated as low as twenty percent)—to the question, "Should the lands forthwith be sold?"

On September 14, 1779, Benson moved to delay the sale of forfeited lands until the next meeting of the legislature.[61] He was supported by Paine and Cooper, opposed by Brinckerhoff, Luddington, Sackett, and Dodge, with the majority. On September 16, accordingly, a bill for immediate sales was reported. A motion was made to delete a provision prohibiting the sale of unimproved lands. It was supported by Brinckerhoff, Luddington, Sackett, and Paine, with the majority; Cooper again joined Benson in opposing it. The bill was then sent back to committee.

The Assembly's readiness, when it reconvened in January, to move from the general to the specific and to consider how and when the forfeited land should be sold, came against the background of a supply crisis in the Army, mounting discontent among the general populace, and the coldest, harshest winter in memory. "The people," wrote future Dutchess Federalist Thomas Tillotson to his brother-in-law Robert R. Livingston in December, "have become very licentious." That same month Margaret Beekman Livingston wrote her son that John DeWitt (the future Anti-Federalist delegate in 1788) was "as arbitrary as a pasha" in assessing taxes; despite the efforts of Tillotson to have the assessment changed, DeWitt had rated her at £1,500 in Rhinebeck and told Tillotson he would tax her Pawling and Beekman holdings too. This was the letter by Margaret Beekman Livingston which ended with the gloomy prophecy of lower-class rule quoted at the beginning of this chapter.[62]

As assemblymen made their way through the heavy snows to Albany, politicians of both parties voiced alarm. "I have not felt equal distress at the situation of our affairs at any period since the commencement of the war," Governor Clinton wrote to Livingston on January 7. "Notwithstanding the great exertions made by the State, it is with the utmost difficulty we feed the troops. . . . They have been frequently days together without bread." Philip Schuyler concurred: "The garrison of Fort Schuyler has been on half allowances, that of Fort George so distressed that they have been on the point of evacuating it." Margaret Beekman Livingston wrote that the people had so little bread she was "apprehensive of a famine." On January 29 the temperature fell to eighteen below zero in Albany. On February 15, John Sloss Hobart wrote to Livingston: "this winter . . . is the most important to us of any that will fall within our age."[63]

On February 4, 1780, the committee having reported that memorials from several counties imploring the speedy sale of lands had been received, the Assembly again voted on whether

to proceed with a bill for immediate sale. Brinckerhoff, Luddington, Sackett, and Paine were in favor, with the majority; Benson
and Dodge opposed.[64]

Benson was then added to the committee working on the bill;
for a short time he now favored the bill. On February 11 and
12 it had its first and second readings. On February 15 an attempt was again made to prevent the sale of unimproved land.
All the Dutchess delegates voted with the overwhelming majority
to reject this motion. On the same day the Dutchess delegation
again unanimously voted for a clause remitting to loyal tenants
all arrearages of rent to the time of the sale of farms. On February 16 it was moved that sequestered farms not be sold if refugees were on them until some other provision was made for them,
or until the end of the war. For the third and last time the Dutchess delegates voted together, with an overwhelming majority, to
defeat the motion.[65]

On February 22 a motion was made to accelerate sales in
certain specified areas, all outside Dutchess County. Brinckerhoff, Sackett, and Paine were in favor, Benson and Dodge
against.[66] On February 28, Benson supported, and Brinckerhoff
and Sackett opposed, a clause to prohibit the sale of lands for
any other purpose than supplying the troops.[67]

Now accepted by the Assembly, the bill met opposition in
the Senate. On March 10 the upper house urged that the sales
of lands should be postponed until further attempts to raise
money by loans had been made. On this, the final Assembly vote,
Benson joined John Jay's brother in supporting the Senate
suggestion, while Brinckerhoff, Sackett, and Dodge joined the
now-victorious majority to reject. On March 11, 1780, the Senate
bowed and the bill became law.[68]

Behind Benson stood Robert R. Livingston, as behind Brinckerhoff stood the Dutchess committees. Benson, the commanding
figure in the Assembly at this time,[69] was obliged to steer a
middle course between the demands of the popular party and the

rugged negatives of his landlord patrons. Livingston had complained to Jay the preceding April:

> Never was there a greater compound of folly avarice and injustice
> than our confiscation bill owing to Bensons *compromising* opinions
> ["and Scotts desire to satisfy the ship carpenters of Poughkeepsie"
> crossed out in original; the "ship carpenters" were Gilbert Living-
> ston and Peter Tappen, who were building boats for the Army].
> Many preparatory steps were taken to produce a change in the dele-
> gations which will take effect shortly.

In this same pattern were Benson's wavering but ultimately nega-
tive course on the bill to sell Loyalist estates, just described, and
his decision to support the price control he so much detested. Yet
when the session ended, Benson as bitterly as Livingston deplored
the split among the Whigs, writing that the session had

> been the most disagreeable and troublesome one I have known;
> almost a continual wrangle from first to last. It certainly is the first
> in which I have known either men or measures lay under the im-
> putation of disaffection. At our first sessions the debate ran high . . .
> but we still believed each other Whigs and so far there was a perfect
> confidence; at the last meeting however our proceedings were poi-
> soned by a distrust, and without cause, if not of Toryism at least
> of cool dispirited Whiggism, equally injurious.[70]

And like Livingston, Benson set himself to change the com-
plexion of the Assembly to one more agreeable.[71]

Although the Council of Revision had warned that "all the
property to be sold under this bill must be sold into the hands
of a few speculators," several of the bill's provisions were designed to keep this from happening. The land was to be sold in
parcels generally of five hundred acres or less, a figure not too
much larger than the one hundred to two hundred acres typical
of farms in the state.[72] Tenants presently in possession were to
have first chance at acquiring their farms.[73] This important fea-
ture of the bill is thus summarized by Yoshpe:

> In the interest of those tenants who had "at considerable expense
> made or purchased the improvements" on the lands in their pos-

session and who had "constantly, uniformly and zealously . . . endeavored to maintain and defend the freedom and independence of the United States," the Commissioners were to offer them preemption of their lands at an appraised price. Until the fee simple of such lands was sold, the tenants were to continue in possession at their former rents. Three appraisers, one chosen by the Commissioners, another by the tenant claiming the benefit intended by this clause, and the third by the other two appraisers, were to evaluate the property "exclusive of the improvements thereon." When the tenant had paid into the treasury the sum at which the lands were appraised, "within three months after the making of such appraisements,"[74] together with all arrearages of rent due thereon, the Commissioners of Forfeitures were to convey the appraised land to such tenant "in like manner as if such lands had been sold at public vendue, and such tenant had appeared and been the highest bidder for the same." Tenants availing themselves of this benefit of preemption of purchase were obliged to produce a certificate, "to be subscribed by at least twelve reputable inhabitants of the county, of known and undoubted attachment to the American cause," testifying that they had "constantly and uniformly" demeaned themselves as friends to the freedom and independence of the United States, and had, as far as circumstances would admit, taken "an active and decided part to maintain and promote the same." [75]

So ran the letter of the law. How was it carried out? Considerable controversy exists among historians as to whether the democratic intention of the law was fulfilled, or whether, after all, speculators took the lion's share of the spoils.[76] The Dutchess evidence indicates that a very large number, probably about half, of the south Dutchess tenants obtained ownership of their farms. Furthermore, taken together with Yoshpe's similar conclusion with respect to the Loyalist estates in Westchester,[77] the Dutchess evidence suggests a new conclusion about the confiscation process in the state as a whole, namely, that where a large, compact, aggressive tenantry existed on a forfeited estate, there the speculator found only marginal pickings. It was small, scattered, uninhabited or urban parcels which lent themselves to speculative operations.

74

Of the 496 forfeited lots in Dutchess County sold under the law, 455 were in southern Dutchess and 414 had belonged to Beverly Robinson or Roger Morris.[78] Charles Inglis had owned 16 lots in Charlotte Precinct, Henry Clinton had owned 41 lots in that part of the Oblong adjoining the Philipse Patent on the east. Thus 471 of the 496 lots had belonged to four men.

The 414 lots in south Dutchess which had belonged to Robinson and Morris were sold to 401 persons; few purchasers acquired more than one lot. These lots, moreover, were actual farms, almost without exception under the five-hundred-acre limit specified by the law. The average lot price, after prices leveled off in 1782, was under one hundred pounds. And not only were the lots cheap, small, and widely distributed, but the purchasers were very often former tenants actually farming the land at the time of confiscation. Of the 401 purchasers of forfeited farms in south Dutchess, 166 had paid taxes in these precincts in 1777.[79] Of 40 tenants actually in possession of a group of Robinson's lots offered for sale in July 1780,[80] 20 purchased the land that they were farming. Pelletreau is certainly very near the mark in his conclusion that "in a large number of cases, in fact a majority, the lands were sold to the parties who were already in possession of the various farms, as tenants of Beverly Robinson and Roger Morris . . ."[81]

The substantially democratic character of the distribution of Loyalist lands in Dutchess is the clue to its significance in county politics. By adding 400 new freeholders to the 1,800 with which Dutchess entered the Revolution, the confiscation law enormously strengthened the voting support of the men who in 1788 would become Anti-Federalists. No wonder that they saw opportunity in the step to which necessity drove them, for these new voting freeholders would be indebted to the legislators who enfranchised them. No wonder that Benson fought the bill step by step through the legislature, that Hamilton set his potent hand to undoing its consequences. For henceforth the conservatives could return to power not by winning elections, but only by circumventing the electoral process. Radical leaders like Mathew Patterson, John Lamb, Zephaniah Platt, John Morin Scott, Jacobus Swartwout, Melancton Smith, and Samuel Jones all picked up one or more of the forfeited Dutchess farms,[82] but their political profit from the law was no less significant than their economic gain.

The continuing political significance of the confiscation law in the seventeen-eighties lay partly in the fact that sales in Dutchess went on till 1786, but stemmed still more from the threat of mortgage foreclosure which hung over the erstwhile-tenant purchaser. It was usually necessary for the tenant to mortgage his land in order to buy it,[83] and mortgage lenders like Robert G. Livingston waited hopefully for the ripe fruits to drop into their hands. As in Westchester, many tenant purchasers "were obliged to encumber their holdings with mortgages in order to raise the money needed for the discharge of their debts,"[84] so many a Dutchess tenant escaped from the clutches of the landlord only to fall into those of the moneylender. Robert G. Livingston was both. Henry G. Livingston, Robert's son and partner, wrote to Gilbert Livingston on March 4, 1781:

> I received a letter from my father Saturday, desiring me to acquaint you that he had a mortgage on the farm late the property of Abraham Payne amounting to about £300. The commissioners sold it to Payne who not being able to make payment was obliged to leave it. They hired it to one Umsted, whose time expires in May next. Then Colonel [name illegible] is to have it. [name illegible] had likewise a mortgage on it and obtained possession I think of this Payne. For farther intelligence please apply to this Payne, who is now at Poughkeepsie a member of Assembly. My father imagines by writing a line to Captain Bloom it may prove of service as he is one of the commissioners. Umsted will hire it of my father.[85]

Several further letters mention this farm but we do not hear who ultimately obtained it. The end of the wartime demand for wheat and the falling price of wheat through the seventeen-eighties [86] must have pressed hard on men who had floated indebtedness in flush times. It was perfectly possible for a mortgaged freeholder to slip back into tenancy.[87] The volume of sheriff's sales and mortgage foreclosures are difficult even to estimate,[88] but the fear of them was certainly widespread.

Once again it is only from their petitions that we know of the tenants' feelings, in this case their desperate struggle to get and keep possession of their farms. Several petitions of tenants who had made a deposit on their farms but could not meet the installment payments are in the New York Assembly Papers.[89] Many of these petitioners were so short of cash in the middle seventeen-eighties that they asked to pay a portion of their payments in wheat or beef. Another, particularly impressive, group of petitions protest the requirement of the law that all back rents be paid before a tenant come into possession of a confiscated farm. "By law," explained the tenants,

> they are obliged either to purchase, or quit their different houses and lands on which they have liv'd for a number of years, which by their industry is brought to some degree of perfection [and] in which consists their little all. Thrice happy would they be, if their circumstances did admit their buying their dwelling, but such is the case, a very few excepted, that were they to sell every thing they own, nay even borrow of their friends, they could not get a sufficient sum to pay for their places.

The petitioners pointed out that they had no alternative "but buying the lands or be turned out of their homes. . . . They would be content in being tenants to the state whereby they could raise grain and provisions to supply our army." This petition, signed by 94 persons, was dated June 1781. In March 1782, 164 persons, all again from Philipstown and Frederickstown in south Dutchess, sent in petitions expressing the same cry of distress.[90] The unpaid back rents of Beverly Robinson's tenants on May 1, 1777, totaled two-and-a-half times their annual rent bill—a good indication of the burden to which the petitioning tenants referred.[91] No doubt partly as a result of these petitions, a law of

April 14, 1782 (5th Session, Ch. 45) permitted half of back rents due to be paid in securities rather than specie.

Thus, even if the Revolution had wiped out tenancy in Dutchess completely, McCracken's conclusion that "Dutchess Clintonianism had nothing to do with tenancy" [92] would hardly be justified. The tenant's dependence on a landlord might become the freeholder's dependence on a moneylender, but the fact of dependence and insecurity remained. After 1779, county politics reverted to the alignment of 1768. Future Anti-Federalists like Swartwout and Gilbert Livingston, and old popular leaders like Brinckerhoff, were opposed as they struggled for price-fixing and confiscation by future Federalist Egbert Benson, who said in 1779 that "for two years past, the Whigs have done the State more damage than the Tories." [93]

And the Revolution did not wipe out tenancy in Dutchess. Two thirds of the farms on the Philipse Patent (the third belonging to Philip Philipse was not sequestered) and a scattering elsewhere in the county had become freeholds. But the stronghold of Federalism in the north had remained predominantly in leasehold. Philip Smith wrote of Northeast Precinct in the eighteen-seventies:

> A considerable portion of this and the adjoining town of Pine Plains is held by leasehold tenure . . . sometimes for life, but more generally for periods of but one year. Of course a tenant has not the same incentive to improve the land as he would have if owner of the soil; as a result the farms are greatly impoverished, and many places are nearly worthless. Many of the houses are badly out of repair, and hardly tenable, and the vicinity wears an aspect of neglect and desolation. The barns and out-buildings are not unfrequently thatched with straw, with doors broken from their hinges, all bearing the impress of age. In a few cases the tenant makes a good livelihood; but in the majority of instances he can barely provide subsistence for his family, to say nothing of rent. Sometimes, rather than leave the place, the tenant will mortgage his stock, in the hope that something will turn up in his favor; but he

78

not infrequently finds himself at the end of the year stripped of his goods and turned out into the street.[94]

Indeed, of 3,400 occupied rural farm units in the county in 1939, 1,391 were tenant-occupied; the Depression can hardly have accounted for all of this.[95] So while distinguished Dutchess antiquarians tell us "the Revolution abolished the leasehold system,"[96] the truth is that "Dutchess County . . . presented a checkered pattern of land tenure with numerous leaseholds interspersed among the predominant freeholds."[97]

The survival of Dutchess landlordism after the Revolution is colorfully illustrated by that hardy perennial, Robert G. Livingston. Livingston had been a Tory; when the British fleet sailed up the Hudson to Kingston and burned the manor houses of Rhinebeck, his alone was left conspicuously untouched. During the war, Robert and his son, Henry, carried on business somewhat gingerly. Thus Henry wrote to Gilbert in 1782:

> In my last to you I requested you to enter on French's farms. I meant to have an ejectment served. The other [suits?] are rather disagreeable I would not wish to have any concern in it at these times.[98]

Robert collected his rents by means of newspaper advertisements which directed his tenants where and whom to pay; it cannot have been a successful method, because one notice addresses itself "to those tenants in arrears, from four, eight or ten years in particular."[99]

With the coming of peace, however, the Livingstons took the oath of loyalty[100] and were, so to speak, back at the old stand. Here are some of their letters of the seventeen-eighties:

> I have wrote several letters to William Devine who bought the farm of William Hammil in Nine Partners. I have his bond and mortgage of £234.3.0 on which I've never had a copper. He has had above three years. I must order him to be arrested please to write him a line threaten him perhaps that may prevail on him to do something.[101]

Dirck has run off and left his son in possession, Dirck has no lease neither has he a promise of one, he owes at least has lived on the farm ten years and paid no rent, the farm in that time has lost all its timber and is now in scandalous condition, its not in his power to pay any rent, and if it was he does not seem inclined to do it. Poppy [Robert G. Livingston] desired me to turn him off as he used him ill by sending him insolent messages such as refusing him rent and saying he would pay to the King etc. etc.[102]

On August 5, 1788, Henry Livingston was to feast five hundred of his Dover neighbors on roast ox to celebrate the ratification of the Constitution by New York.[103]

The basis for pre-Revolutionary politics therefore remained. In January 1781, almost a year after the law enacting the sale of Loyalist estates, Robert R. Livingston was writing to Gouverneur Morris that "the people are clamorous; the whole county of Dutchess have chosen precinct and county committees to instruct their members." In the same month he wrote to George Washington of the popular grievances that "sore and dissatisfied their discontents begin to break out in complaints against their rulers in committees and instructions."[104] In December of that year, Margaret Beekman Livingston wrote her son that "wheat continues at the low price of 5/ [shillings a bushel]. I know not what will become of our farmers." [105] Six months later another Dutchess Federalist-to-be, Tillotson, looked out over the troubled seas of post-Revolutionary politics with foreboding. New York, he wrote Livingston,

> has a strong democratic spirit prevailing that will some day not far off give a stab to its happiness. . . . The people want nothing but to be a little more impoverished to prepare them for it. The first stroke will be at the tenanted estates.[106]

As we try to imagine the Dutchess farmer viewing the Constitutional struggle, I think we must see him concerned not so much about the price of wheat, or the rate of taxes, as about preserving the economic and political independence so recently and painfully acquired. The Constitution's promoters, in his eyes, were a class of men almost hereditary enemies in many parts of Dutchess. The Constitution's opponents, prosperous and self-interested though they might be, had nonetheless sponsored a new distribution of power based on a new distribution of land. What Crevecoeur said of Europe—

> a country that has no bread for him, whose fields procured him no harvest, who met nothing but the frowns of the rich, the severity of the laws, with jails and punishments; who owned not a single foot of the extensive surface of this planet [107]

—had been America for the farmer of south Dutchess. What his philosophical Ulster neighbor thought were the inevitable fruits of emigration—

> he now feels himself a man, because he is treated as such . . . Judge what an alteration must arise in the mind and thoughts of this man; he begins to forget his former servitude and dependence, his heart involuntarily swells and glows; this first swell inspires him with those new thoughts which constitute an American [108]

—the Dutchess tenant had had to wrest by revolution.

RHETORIC AND REALITY

AT POUGHKEEPSIE

The study of Anti-Federalism in Dutchess County must end at the Poughkeepsie courthouse, where the New York ratifying convention, meeting from the middle of June to the end of July 1788, gave the county its one brief moment of greatness in American history.

The story of the convention is a familiar one: How the delegates gathered on June 17, with onlookers crowding the courthouse galleries; how each evening the contending factions retired to their respective inns to lay plans for the coming day; how on July 2, Hamilton's messenger broke all standing speed records between New York City and Poughkeepsie to bring the news that Virginia had ratified; and how, finally, a dozen Anti-Federalist delegates, headed by Smith, Platt, Livingston, and DeWitt of Dutchess, crossed the floor of the house to bring New York also into the new Union.

The defection of these four men not only provided the numerical margin for the Federalists' thirty to twenty-seven victory; it was the more significant because Smith and Livingston had been two of the principal Anti-Federalist orators in the convention's first weeks. When they reversed their field, Gilbert Livingston might call it the most difficult decision of his life,[1] but there is no mistaking the cutting way in which the die-hard Anti-Federalists referred to their erstwhile allies in the closing days of the debate.[2] Beyond any doubt, could we understand why the Dutchess delegation divided, and why four delegates chose one side and two the other,[3] the reasons for New York's ratification would be much more clear.

The records of the convention tell tantalizingly little. It is plain that after the news of ratification by New Hampshire and Virginia, Smith proposed one compromise formula after another, each one a little closer to the Federalist position.[4] He himself stated that, after Virginia ratified, he decided amendments could best be secured if New York joined rather than rejected the Union.[5] Livingston and Platt justified their votes only by generalities,[6] while Swartwout and Akin—the two Dutchess delegates voting "Nay"—said not one recorded word. The evidence is long on speechmaking and almost nonexistent as to the behind-the-scenes maneuvers which must have been decisive.

Yet in the context of Dutchess politics throughout the Revolutionary era, two facts of the convention stand out in a new light. While by no means do they altogether clarify the convention behavior of the Dutchess delegates, they do take us a good deal further along the road.

One of these facts is the extraordinary speech on the size of the House of Representatives delivered by Melancton Smith on

83

June 21: extraordinary because it summarized so precisely the politics of Dutchess County in the Revolutionary generation. "By increasing the number of representatives," Smith said,

> we open a door for the admission of the substantial yeomanry of our country. . . . The knowledge necessary for the representative of a free people not only comprehends extensive political and commercial information, such as is obtained by men of refined education, who have leisure to obtain to high degrees of improvement, but it should also comprehend that kind of acquaintance with the common concerns and occupations of the people, which men of the middling class of life are, in general, more competent to than those of a superior class. . . . the influence of the great will generally enable them to succeed in elections. It will be difficult to combine a district of country containing thirty or forty thousand inhabitants—frame your election laws as you please—in any other character, unless it be in one of conspicuous military, popular, civil, or legal talents. The great easily form associations; the poor and middling class form them with difficulty. . . . There will be scarcely a chance of their uniting in any other but some great man, unless in some popular demagogue, who will probably be destitute of principle. A substantial yeoman, of sense and discernment, will hardly ever be chosen.

"The great," Smith continued,

> do not feel for the poor and middling class; the reasons are obvious—they are not obliged to use the same pains and labor to procure property as the other. They feel not the inconveniences arising from the payment of small sums. The great consider themselves above the common people, entitled to more respect, do not associate with them; they fancy themselves to have a right of preeminence in every thing. In short, they possess the same feelings, and are under the influence of the same motives, as an hereditary nobility. . . . We ought to guard against the government being placed in the hands of this class. They cannot have that sympathy with their constituents which is necessary to connect them closely with their interests.[7]

This speech was rhetoric, a knitting-together of the themes of Anti-Federalist propaganda into a single image of the ratification struggle. In my view it was also, like the Tenth Federalist Paper as interpreted by Beard, a substantially accurate statement of "how it really was."

To be sure, Smith's "respectable yeomanry" were not indigent tenants. They were the "middling class" from which the typical Anti-Federalist politician, but not the typical Anti-Federalist voter, was drawn; Smith revealed this in a later reference to "the middling class of people . . . such as compose the body of this assembly."[8] Smith had in mind well-to-do farmers like Brinckerhoff and Van Kleek, who defeated two Livingstons in 1768; men like George Clinton, who, in Chancellor Livingston's words, "was not promoted to the chief magistracy for his riches, but his virtue";[9] men, indeed, like that "Messr. Melancton Smith" who had taken his place with so many esquires in the Dutchess delegation to the First Provincial Congress.

But it would be quite wrong to conclude that these prosperous Anti-Federalist leaders were no better democrats than their opponents. This is to make Beard's mistake of taking the individual leader in focus and neglecting his constituency. For the Brinckerhoffs and Van Kleeks, the Clintons and the Smiths, had indeed been more responsive to the distress of small men and tenants than were Jay or Benson, Duane or Robert Livingston. The change from Philip Livingston to Melancton Smith, from Beverly Robinson to Ephraim Paine, had been a change indeed. Chancellor Livingston must have cut very little ice at the convention when, in rebuttal to Smith, he said, "I hope, sir, we are all aristocrats."[10]

Thus, Smith's speech illustrates one of the principal conclusions of this study: that the binding element of Anti-Federalism in Dutchess County, the thing which all the Anti-Federalists at Poughkeepsie had in common, was hostility to the aristocratic landlord families. Between 1777 and 1788 not one member of the old ruling families held an important elective or appointive position in Dutchess County.

A second fact illuminated by the history of the politics of Dutchess County before 1788 is the way the Dutchess delegation at the convention divided. Of the county's seven delegates, the two who voted against the Constitution were Jacobus Swartwout and Jonathan Akin from south Dutchess, whereas the four who voted "Aye" were all from the neighborhood of Poughkeepsie. In this the behavior of Dutchess delegates at the convention anticipated the pattern of county voting in the seventeen-nineties, when south Dutchess was consistently Clintonian and central Dutchess wavered.

Apart from the attitudes of their constituents, the families of both Swartwout and Akin had been directly involved in the tenant disturbances of 1766. Quite possibly it was Jacobus Swartwout himself [11] who took the Indian lease described in the following letter from Catherine Brett (who claimed to own the land) to Sir William Johnson:

> Some mischievous white people went to the Indians and hired little bits of land and made them give them leases, then they put in what quantity of land they pleased and made their leases for ninety-nine years. And this old Nimham has been dead about twelve years but his children might have stayed on till this day but his oldest son one Shake came to me and asked me liberty to sell the improvement to one Captain Swartwout. I opposed it at first and a little after he came down again with seven or eight more Indians for liberty to sell the improvement. I gave him leave to sell the improvement and he sold it for twenty pounds. It being a precarious time, I suffered all this, for fear of their setting up the Indians against me.[12]

As to the Akins, they owned land in two of the disputed "gores" near Quaker Hill and Patterson, as mentioned above. But their connection with the tenant rising was closer than this. For the father (also named Jonathan Akin) of the Jonathan Akin of 1788 was one of the two justices of the peace who legally confirmed Samuel Munroe's status as attorney for the Wappinger Indians. What this action signified is indicated by a report to the

governor in council, in March 1765, which said of the two justices that their behavior

> appears to this committee such an abuse of their respective offices,
> and so dangerous a precedent for encouraging Indian claims
> against the rights of the Crown, and in disinherison of his Majesty,
> that the committee is humbly of opinion, that an order of your honor
> in council ought to be served on the said Terboss and Akins, for
> them to show cause why they should not be displaced for such
> misconduct.[13]

As a result, both Akin and Terboss were "excused" from the
commission of the peace in 1766.[14]

We catch one other glimpse of Akin at this time. At the trial
of Prendergast in August 1766, he testified that he had persuaded
a group of the rioters to give up their guns.[15] That he gave this
advice, and that he was trusted enough to be persuasive, ex-
presses in capsule form the relation of the Dutchess Anti-Federalist leaders to the men they represented. It is altogether mistaken
to conceive the leveling aspirations of the Revolution as a figment
of the Federalist imagination.[16] But it is equally essential to
realize that the Anti-Federalist leaders were sunshine radicals
and summer subversives, if they were really radicals and subversives at all.

The division of the Dutchess delegation at Poughkeepsie,
therefore, points to the study's second major conclusion: the
existence of a characteristic divergence of aim between leaders
and constituents within the Anti-Federalist party. The typical
Anti-Federalist leader in Dutchess was a man of the "middling
class" who lived in a neighborhood which had long enjoyed the
security of freehold tenure. Many, if not most, of the county's
Anti-Federalist voters were men for whom tenancy was an ever-
present reality, or fear; many also were accustomed to collective
direct action above and beyond the political forms more natural
to their representatives. A tendency to compromise was, so to
speak, built right into the socio-economic world of the leaders,

whereas a latent extremism was just as naturally built into that of the voters.

The judicially minded reader may object that these conclusions rest wholly on circumstantial evidence. True enough, precinct election statistics are missing, the heritage of tenant troubles has not been proven relevant to 1788, the class-conscious statements in the press and at the convention can be dismissed as propaganda. Yet the evidence presented in the course of the foregoing study would appear, although circumstantial, to possess a certain cumulative authority. As R. G. Collingwood remarks, there are "people who, if they met you one Saturday afternoon with a fishing-rod, creel, and campstool, walking towards the river, would ask, 'Going fishing?' "

NOTES

INTRODUCTION

[1] Charles A. Beard, *An Economic Interpretation of the Constitution of the United States* (New York, 1913), pp. 19, 22, 24.

[2] Robert E. Brown, *Charles Beard and the Constitution: A Critical Analysis of "An Economic Interpretation of the Constitution"* (Princeton, 1956); Forrest McDonald, *We, The People: The Economic Origins of the Constitution* (Chicago, 1958).

[3] An example: McDonald in his discussion of New York states as simple facts that the Anti-Federalists at the ratifying convention caucused on July 25 and decided that three of their number should vote for ratification, and that this alleged decision was influenced by the threat of Federalist southern New York to secede (McDonald, *We, The People*, p. 288). In reality, conclusive evidence has not been discovered for either assertion.

[4] Oran Libby, "The Geographical Distribution of the Vote of the Thirteen States on the Federal Constitution, 1787-8," *Bulletin of the University of Wisconsin: Economics, Political Science, and History*, Series I (Madison, 1897), p. 18.

[5] Expressions of this tendency are Oscar and Mary Handlin, "Radicals and Conservatives in Massachusetts after Independence," *New England Quarterly*, XVII (September 1944), 343-55; Robert E. Brown, *Middle-Class Democracy and the Revolution in Massachusetts, 1691-1780* (Ithaca, 1955); Richard B.

Morris, "The Confederation Period and the American Historian," *William and Mary Quarterly*, 3d series, XIII (April 1956), 139-56; Edmund S. Morgan, "The American Revolution: Revisions in Need of Revising," *ibid.*, 3d series, XIV (January 1957), 3-15.

6 Carl Becker, *The History of Political Parties in the Province of New York, 1760-1776* (Madison, 1909).

7 Handlin and Handlin, "Radicals and Conservatives," p. 355.

8 Merrill Jensen, *The New Nation: A History of the United States during the Confederation, 1781-1789.* (New York, 1950).

9 McDonald, *We, The People*, p. 405.

10 Lee Benson, "A Critique of Beard and his Critics" (unpublished), pp. 126-27. The study of the English Civil War has run into the identical problem in recent years. Painstaking research on the members of the Long Parliament has shown few characteristic differences in occupation or financial status between Cavalier and Roundhead M.P.'s (D. Brunton and D. H. Pennington, *Members of the Long Parliament* [London, 1954]). Yet there can be no doubt that the strength of Parliament was concentrated in certain regions (the South and East) and that of the king in others (the North and West). Likewise, no matter how many studies of the ratifying conventions show that Anti-Federalist delegates invested in government securities as heavily as Federalist delegates, it will remain true that Libby demonstrated a definite overall pattern in the geographic distribution of Federalist and Anti-Federalist voters. Both in England and America, the differences between parties apparently need to be sought in their constituencies, rather than in their leaders. See also Chapter 2, note 66, below.

11 Robert E. Thomas, "The Virginia Convention of 1788: A Criticism of Beard's *An Economic Interpretation of the Constitution*," *Journal of Southern History*, XIX (February 1953), 72.

12 Jackson T. Main, "Sections and Politics in Virginia, 1781-1787," *William and Mary Quarterly*, 3d series, XII (January 1955), 96-112.

13 A biased but pioneering study is Cecilia M. Kenyon, "Men of Little Faith: The Anti-Federalists on the Nature of Representative Government," *ibid.*, 3d series, XII (January 1955), 3-43.

14 William Smith, *History of New York from the First Discovery to . . . 1762* (New York, 1830), I, 311.

15 *Heads of Families at the First Census of the United States Taken in the Year 1790—New York* (Washington, 1908), p. 9.

CHAPTER I

1 Peter Tappen to George Clinton, September 29, 1787, Bancroft Transcripts, New York Public Library.

2 *Country Journal and Poughkeepsie Advertiser*, October 3, 1787 (hereafter referred to as *Country Journal*).

3 Charles E. Benton, *Troutbeck: A Dutchess County Homestead* (Poughkeepsie, 1916), p. 13.

[4] John Theodore Horton, *James Kent: A Study in Conservatism, 1763-1847* (New York, c. 1939), p. 57; *Country Journal*, June 3, 1788.

[5] Lamb Papers, Box 5, New York Historical Society.

[6] *Country Journal*, April 8, 1788.

[7] The fullest account is Clarence E. Miner, *The Ratification of the Federal Constitution by the State of New York* (New York, 1921).

[8] Albany Anti-Federalist Committee to John Lamb, April 12, 1788, Lamb Papers, Box 5.

[9] Quoted by Kenneth Pickthorn, *Early Tudor Government: Henry VII* (Cambridge, 1934), p. 103.

[10] *Country Journal*, March 18, 1788. See also "Cato" in *ibid.*, December 12, 1787, who accused the Anti-Federalists of wishing to set all servants and apprentices free.

[11] *Ibid.*, April 8, 1788.

[12] Merrill Jensen, *The Articles of Confederation* (Madison, 1940), pp. 244, 241. Anti-Federalists regularly identified themselves with "the spirit of '76," for example in the letter to the *Country Journal*, January 16, 1788, beginning: "You will oblige one whose whiggism as well as ideas of liberty, were fashionable in 75, 76 and 77 . . .."

[13] *Country Journal*, March 4, 1788.

[14] *Ibid.*

[15] *Ibid.*, March 18, 1788.

[16] *Ibid.*, April 8, 1788.

[17] Brown, *Charles Beard and the Constitution*, p. 21.

[18] Richard Hofstadter, "Beard and the Constitution: The History of an Idea," *American Quarterly*, II (Fall 1950), Part 3.

[19] Beard, *An Economic Interpretation*, p. 325.

[20] Universal manhood suffrage was stipulated in the New York legislature's bill establishing a ratifying convention. It did not become a part of the state's regular election procedure until the eighteen-twenties. The secret ballot in Assembly elections had begun in 1787 (E. Wilder Spaulding, *New York in the Critical Period, 1783-1789* [New York, 1932], p. 89). Local polling places were enacted on March 27, 1788, just one month before the election (Franklin B. Hough, *The New York Civil List* [Albany, 1861], pp. 107 n., 118).

[21] Spaulding, *New York, 1783-1789*, pp. 200-01.

[22] The New York constitution of 1777 required a freehold of one hundred pounds in voting for governor and state senators, and a twenty-pound freehold or a tenement renting for forty shillings a year in voting for assemblymen. One authority believes that in practice "only paupers and lodgers or sons living with their parents" were excluded from voting for assemblymen (Alexander Flick, editor, *The American Revolution in New York* [Albany, 1926], p. 91). The New York electoral census of 1790 (*New York Daily Advertiser*, January 15, 1791) indicates that less than one third of the free white males over sixteen were qualified to vote for governor.

[23] *New York Historical and Genealogical Register*, II (January 1871), 149-50.

[24] The free white male population over sixteen in Poughkeepsie Precinct in 1790 was 617 (*Heads of Families at the First Census*, p. 9).

25 "The opposition . . . suffered from the difficulties connected with getting a back-woods vote out to the town and county elections. This involved sometimes long journeys in bad weather" (Beard, *An Economic Interpretation*, p. 252). See also Becker, *History of Political Parties*, p. 15.

26 Becker, *History of Political Parties*, p. 17. It should not be assumed that the traditional pressure of landlords on tenants disappeared completely. For such pressure from the Livingstons in the 1787-1788 elections in Columbia County and in the 1789 elections in Dutchess County, see Robert Livingston to James Duane, April 30, 1788, Duane Papers, New York Historical Society; Thomas Tillotson to Robert R. Livingston, March 23, 1787, and Margaret Beekman Livingston to Robert R. Livingston, April 1789, Robert R. Livingston Papers, New York Historical Society.

27 *Country Journal*, June 3, 1788.

28 James Hughes to John Lamb, June 18, 1788, Lamb Papers, Box 5.

CHAPTER II

1 Benson's sister, Tryntje, married into another Rhinebeck Federalist family, the Hoffmans (Dutchess County Historical Society, *Yearbook*, VIII [1923], 54). Hereafter the Dutchess County Historical Society *Yearbook* will be referred to as D.C.H.S., *Yearbook*.

2 Philip L. White, *The Beekmans of New York in Politics and Commerce, 1647-1877* (New York, 1956), p. 159.

3 Joan Gordon, "Kinship and Class: The Livingstons of New York, 1675-1860" (unpublished Ph.D. thesis, Columbia University, 1959), p. 189.

4 Henry Noble McCracken, *Old Dutchess Forever! The Story of an American County* (New York, 1956), Chapter 11.

5 Richard Smith, *A Tour of Four Great Rivers: The Hudson, Mohawk, Susque-hanna and Delaware in 1769*, edited by Francis W. Halsey (New York, 1906), p. 10.

6 Philip H. Smith, *General History of Dutchess County from 1609 to 1876 Inclusive* (New York, 1877), p. 383.

7 Harry Arnold, "Reminiscences of the Lewis Estate at Staatsburgh," D.C.H.S., *Yearbook*, XIII (1928), 33-35. In 1762, Judge Robert Livingston of Clermont wrote his son, the future chancellor, that he had "let 8 farms of 100 acres . . . for the 10th of all grain and each farm to ride and boards from the saw mill which is a higher rent than any in Dutchess County" (letter of March 12, 1762, Robert R. Livingston Papers).

8 H. W. Reynolds, "D'Cantillon's Landing," D.C.H.S., *Yearbook*, XXV (1940), 77, 82.

9 Philip Smith, *General History*, pp. 223-24.

10 A tenant whose lease ran for twenty-one years or more was a freeholder for voting purposes. Cadwallader Colden wrote Lord Dartmouth in 1775 that there were enough freeholders within the manors of Livingston and Rensselaer to control the elections of Albany County (Becker, *History of Political Parties*, p. 11).

11 The Committee of Albany to John Lamb, April 12, 1788, Lamb Papers, Box 5.

12 Henry G. Livingston to Gilbert Livingston, January 1, 1782, Gilbert Livingston Papers, Box 1, New York Public Library: "The law respecting twenty-one years was artfully inserted to prevent the landlords' influence over tenants, as a lease for twenty-one years did not entitle a tenant to vote for Governor."

13 "A particular list or description of each dwelling-house . . . possessed or occupied on the first day of October, 1798, in Rhynbeck Town," Gilbert Livingston Land Papers, New York Public Library. See Chapter 1, note 26, above, for instances of election pressure by the Livingstons.

14 See McCracken, *Old Dutchess Forever*, pp. 447, 464, 472: "Gradually, out of the welter of opinion, there emerged a Northern and Central Dutchess Federalism that stuck through thick and thin, while the south supported George Clinton and Democratic Republicanism against the landlords." If one takes the ratio of one-hundred-pound freeholders to adult white males as a rough indication of socio-economic status, it is significant that the only two Dutchess townships in which this ratio was over thirty percent were strongly Federalist in the congressional election of 1790 and throughout most of the decade, while the only two townships in which this ratio was under twenty percent were Philipstown and Frederickstown—the scene of the 1766 tenant riots and of the bulk of confiscated Loyalist lands (Chapters 3 and 4, below)—which were Clintonian in 1790 and 1792. For the returns by township of the 1790 congressional elections, see the *New York Daily Advertiser*, May 21, 1790.

15 Dixon Ryan Fox, *The Decline of Aristocracy in the Politics of New York* (New York, 1919), p. 35.

16 See Gouverneur Morris to Robert R. Livingston, September 22, 1778, with regard to the New York delegation in the Continental Congress: "If there is any man of the lower orders whom you can trust, a DeWitt for instance, I think it would be advisable to be open-mouthed and loud for him. Such a man would be of infinite service if appointed by US" (Robert R. Livingston Papers).

17 Troy (New York) Times, *The Past and Present of Plattsburgh* (Troy, 1891), p. 2 and following.

18 Livingston's account book in the Library of Congress, cited by Horton, *James Kent*, p. 51 n.

19 Gordon, "Kinship and Class," p. 197, based on the Gilbert Livingston Land Papers.

20 H. W. Reynolds, "James Kent," D.C.H.S., *Yearbook*, VIII (1923), 23, quoting Kent's letter to William B. Reed in 1847; Gordon, "Kinship and Class," p. 199.

21 McDonald, *We, The People*, p. 307.

22 J. Wilson Poucher, "Smith Thompson," D.C.H.S., *Yearbook*, XXV (1940), 26.

23 Elinor Beckwith, "Highlights in the History of the Town of Stanford," *ibid.*, XXXVII (1952), 24.

24 "DeWitt Family," *ibid.*, II (1915-1916), 34-36.

25 Amanda Akin Stearns, *Ancient Homes and Early Days of Quaker Hill* (Quaker Hill, 1903), p. 22 and following.

26 Tax Lists, 1771-1779, Adriance Memorial Library, Poughkeepsie.

27 Compiled from the tax list printed in William Pelletreau, *History of Putnam County, New York* (Philadelphia, 1886), p. 121 and following.

28 Robert A. East, *Business Enterprise in the American Revolutionary Era* (New

York, 1938), pp. 94, 108, 117-18, 146, 225, 275, 318. An interesting instance of Melancton Smith's speculative activity is the following letter to him from his brother Israel, then in the Revolutionary Army: "As to procuring any more [soldiers'] certificates I cannot at the price you mention, had I the cash; and those who would part with them do it for no other reason than the want of it. Goods at Albany is too far" (Israel Smith to Melancton Smith, February 21-22, 1782, Lawrence and Smith Papers, New York Historical Society).

29 J. Wilson Poucher, "Peter Tappen," D.C.H.S., *Yearbook*, XIX (1934), 38-44; Amy Van Nooy, "Elizabeth Crannell, Wife of Doctor Peter Tappen," *ibid*., XXXVII (1952), 71; Isaac Huntting, *History of Little Nine Partners of North East Precinct, and Pine Plains, New York* (Amenia, 1897), p. 379; George B. Kinkead, "Gilbert Livingston and Some of his Descendants," *New York Genealogical and Biographical Record*, LXXXVI (1953), 35.

30 "General Jacobus Swartwout," D.C.H.S., *Yearbook*, XIII (1928), 71.

31 H. W. Reynolds, "Frances Filkin's Book," *ibid*., XXIII (1938), 52-71.

32 Horton, *James Kent*, p. 44.

33 Edmund Platt, *The Eagle's History of Poughkeepsie* (Poughkeepsie, 1905), p. 54.

34 Van Nooy, "Elizabeth Crannell," p. 74.

35 Milton M. Klein, "Democracy and Politics in Colonial New York," *New York History*, XL (July 1959), 225.

36 Gordon, "Kinship and Class," pp. 264-65.

37 *Ibid*., p. 266 n.

38 Gilbert was Dutchess County surrogate in 1778-1785, 1787-1804 (Hough, *The New York Civil List*, p. 457).

39 Willis Johnson, *Colonel Henry Luddington: A Memoir* (New York, 1907), pp. 38-39.

40 Pelletreau, *Putnam County*, p. 121 and following.

41 Johnson, *Colonel Henry Luddington*, p. 208.

42 "Colonel James Vanderburgh," D.C.H.S., *Yearbook*, XV (1930), 36-44.

43 *Ibid*., p. 36.

44 Stearns, *Ancient Homes*, pp. 10-11, 22 and following.

45 "Colonel James Vanderburgh," pp. 36, 44.

46 Philip Smith, *General History*, p. 448.

47 McCracken, *Old Dutchess Forever*, p. 198.

48 Thus the Baptist congregation of Northeast declared slavery contrary to the Gospel in 1778 (James H. Smith, *History of Dutchess County, New York* [Syracuse, 1882], p. 249).

49 Pelletreau, *Putnam County*, p. 657; Johnson, *Colonel Henry Luddington*, p. 208.

50 *Country Journal*, December 22, 1785.

51 Hough, *The New York Civil List*, p. 117.

52 "Colonel James Vanderburgh"; Pelletreau, *Putnam County*, pp. 367, 630; Johnson, *Colonel Henry Luddington*, p. 203.

53 Hough, *The New York Civil List*, p. 420.

54 *Ibid*., p. 446: They were Melancton Smith (1778-1780), Lewis DuBois (1781-1784), and Harmon Hoffman (1785-1789).

55 Provincial congresses, 1775-1777: Federalists, Anthony Hoffman (delegate to three congresses), James Vanderburgh (one), Joseph Crane (one); Anti-

Federalists, Gilbert Livingston (four), Zephaniah Platt (three), Melancton Smith (one). *Ibid.*, pp. 62-65.

Senate: Federalists, Anthony Hoffman (1788-1790); Anti-Federalists, Zephaniah Platt (1777-1783), Jacobus Swartwout (1784-1795). *Ibid.*, pp. 122-30.

Assembly: Federalists, Egbert Benson (1777-1781, 1788), Anthony Hoffman (1777-1779, 1784), Joseph Crane (1778), Ebeneezer Cary (1780, 1784), Henry Luddington (1779-1780, 1786-1787), Peter Cantine (1788), Thomas Tillotson (1788); Anti-Federalists, Gilbert Livingston (1777), Jacobus Swartwout (1777-1778, 1780-1782), Mathew Patterson (1782-1788), John DeWitt (1786-1788), Lewis DuBois (1786). *Ibid.*, pp. 183-93.

Continental Congress: Federalists, Egbert Benson (October 1781, February 1784, October 1784, January 1787, February 1788); Anti-Federalists, Zephaniah Platt (October 1784, March 1785, February 1786), Melancton Smith (March 1785, February 1786, January 1787). *Ibid.*, p. 74.

56 See note 54. The Federalists were Benson, Cantine, and Tillotson; the Anti-Federalists, Patterson and DeWitt.

57 Federalists: Richard D'Cantillon, supervisor of Clinton, 1787; Wiltse, Rombout, 1780; Tallman, Pawling, 1781-1782; Anthony Hoffman, Rhinebeck, 1781-1785; Peter Cantine, Rhinebeck, 1786-1787; Ebeneezer Cary, Beekman, four years before the Revolution; Joseph Crane, Southeast, 1773, 1781, 1783-1787. Anti-Federalists: Gilbert Livingston, supervisor of Poughkeepsie, 1769 and 1784; Zephaniah Platt, Poughkeepsie, 1772-1776; John Bailey, Poughkeepsie, 1780-1782; Peter Tappen, Poughkeepsie, 1783; Lewis DuBois, Poughkeepsie, 1785-1786; Jacobus Swartwout, Rombout, 1774-1775; Ezra Thompson, Charlotte (later divided into Clinton and Stanford), 1776-1779. Basic list in Frank Hasbrouck, editor, *The History of Dutchess County, New York* (Poughkeepsie, 1909), pp. 62-64; also Louise Hasbrouck Zimm and others, editors, *Southeastern New York: A History of the Counties of Ulster, Dutchess, Orange, Rockland and Putnam* (New York, 1946), I, 274.

58 Instances are given in Pelletreau, *Putnam County*, p. 147 and following.

59 The records of the first Hyde Park town meeting in 1821 say: "the following gentlemen were chosen *viva voce* or by lifting up of hands . . ." (James Smith, *Dutchess County*, p. 303).

60 *Ibid.*, p. 70.

61 Before the Revolution, Beverly Robinson, who owned one third of Frederickstown and Southeast, was often a supervisor, as were Filkins and Stoutenburghs in Crum Elbow Precinct.

62 *Country Journal*, April 8, 1788.

63 Philip Smith, *General History*, pp. 77-78.

64 *Ibid.*, pp. 36-44.

65 *Ibid.*, p. 75.

66 Main, "Sections and Politics," pp. 97-98.

67 Here again an analogy to the English Revolution of the sixteen-forties is instructive. Referring to studies of the revolutionary committees in the counties of Stafford and Kent, Christopher Hill says that in both counties one party "drew its main strength from the old ruling families," while the members of the other party were in general "of markedly inferior social origin" (*Puritanism and*

Revolution: Studies in Interpretation of the English Revolution of the Seventeenth Century [London, 1958], pp. 21-22).

CHAPTER III

1 Alice Curtis Desmond, "Mary Philipse: Heiress," *New York History*, XXVIII (January 1947), 26.
2 Irving Mark, *Agrarian Conflicts in Colonial New York, 1711-1775* (New York, 1940), p. 147.
3 The population of the county in 1713 was 445 (Federal Writers' Project American Guide Series, *Dutchess County* [Philadelphia, 1937], p. 11).
4 Spaulding, *New York, 1783-1789*, p. 53.
5 McCracken, *Old Dutchess Forever*, p. 234.
6 Jennie Green, "Some History and Some Traditions of Pawling, New York," D.C.H.S., *Yearbook*, XXIX (1944), 57.
7 Quoted by James Smith, *Dutchess County*, p. 254.
8 Irving Mark and Oscar Handlin, "Land Cases in Colonial New York, 1765-1767: The King vs. William Prendergast," *New York University Law Review*, XIX (January 1942), 168.
9 Oscar Handlin, "The Eastern Frontier of New York," *New York History*, XVIII (January 1937), 52.
10 McCracken, *Old Dutchess Forever*, p. 73. In the same year Beekman was rated at four hundred pounds.
11 For Rombout, Helen Wilkinson Reynolds, editor, *Eighteenth Century Records of the Portion of Dutchess County, New York, that was included in Rombout Precinct*, Dutchess County Historical Society, Collections, VI (1938), Preface; for Poughkeepsie and Amenia, James Smith, *Dutchess County*, pp. 54, 342; for Charlotte, McCracken, *Old Dutchess Forever*, p. 40.
12 Gilbert Livingston Land Papers. Spaulding wholly misinterprets this material because he believes it to deal with Livingston Manor.

The leases and other legal documents in the Land Papers are valuably supplemented by the correspondence between various Livingstons in the two boxes of the Gilbert Livingston Papers. The letters reveal a bizarre mixture of very hardheaded business instructions with family chitchat. For example, Robert G. Livingston to Gilbert Livingston, September 28, 1786: "Abraham Finch was here two days ago soliciting for further time to pay the small balance remaining, I told him I had waited long enough already and that I would not consent to anything of the kind and am with our kind love to all at the house . . ."; and Henry G. to Gilbert, January 1, 1782: "Inclosed you have two notes against Rufus Herrick have you arrested Shafer? Affectionately . . ." (both in Box 1).
13 Lewis Namier, *The Structure of Politics at the Accession of George III*, second edition (London, 1957), p. 70.
14 *Ibid.*, p. 73.
15 These figures are with one exception derived from O'Callaghan's documents, for example the total of 235 freeholders in 1740 (Report of Sheriff James Wilson,

Documentary History of the State of New York, edited by E. B. O'Callaghan [Albany, 1851], IV, 135-36). The total of 1,800 freeholders in 1775 is from a letter in Peter Force, editor, *American Archives* (Washington, 1837), Series 4, II, 304.

[16] William Smith, above, Introduction, note 14.

[17] Federal Writers' Project, *Dutchess County*, p. 13.

[18] Klein, "Democracy and Politics," p. 237. However, in support of Klein, see Chilton Williamson, *American Suffrage: From Property to Democracy, 1760-1860* (Princeton, 1960), p. 28.

[19] Mark, *Agrarian Conflict*, p. 97 n. Mark conjectures that 10,000 could vote in a total population of 95,000. I have transformed these figures into a percentage of voters to adult males by dividing 95,000 by five.

[20] Charles S. Sydnor, *Gentlemen Freeholders* (Chapel Hill, 1952), pp. 28-32, Appendix II.

[21] Here again the present study supports Becker, who wrote: "It is perhaps safe to say that over half of the male population over the age of twenty-one years" could not vote (*History of Political Parties*, p. 11).

[22] About a dozen letters from 1743 to 1753 are in the Henry Livingston Papers, Franklin Delano Roosevelt Library, Hyde Park; they are printed in "A Packet of Old Letters," D.C.H.S., *Yearbook*, VI (1921), 26-61. Philip White in his biography of the Beekman family draws on other letters in the correspondence from the Beekman Papers of the New York Historical Society.

[23] Beekman to Livingston, May 13, 1752, "A Packet of Old Letters," p. 37.

[24] Beekman to Livingston, December 19, 1751, *ibid.*, p. 34. Other illustrations of Beekman's approach to elections are his request that his son send a list of freeholders with each name marked "Like" or "Dislike," and his report that after talking with some Quaker leaders after church, "they signified that all the Friends would go one way. They can make about 100 votes in our County" (Beekman to his brother, May 9, 1744, and Beekman to Livingston, February 10, 1749, Miscellaneous Manuscripts—Dutchess County, New York Historical Society).

[25] Sydnor, *Gentlemen Freeholders*, Chapter 4.

[26] Beekman to Livingston, January 23, 1752, "A Packet of Old Letters," p. 35.

[27] For Beekman's control of patronage, see White, *Beekmans of New York*, pp. 169-70, 191-92, 183.

[28] *Ibid.*, p. 191.

[29] Beekman to Livingston, May 2, 1743, "A Packet of Old Letters," p. 29.

[30] Beekman to Livingston, November 26, 1747, *ibid.*, p. 33.

[31] James Alexander to Joseph Murray, April 11, 1753, Robert R. Livingston Papers.

[32] Beekman's challengers and their motives are discussed by White, *Beekmans of New York*, pp. 192-98, 206-07.

[33] Beekman to Livingston, December 19, 1751, "A Packet of Old Letters," p. 34. Also, Beekman wrote to Livingston on August 31, 1749, that a riot had occurred on "Sister Pawling's lot" (Miscellaneous Manuscripts—Dutchess County) and on April 7, 1752, that a tenant was claiming "he held under a new fair field right and not under Philips. So that they trump up more and more titles against us" (Henry Livingston Papers).

34 Above, Introduction, note 14.

35 "Four-fifths of the land of Dutchess was not opened for settlement until after 1730" (McCracken, *Old Dutchess Forever*, p. 77). The exact division of a patent among its absentee purchasers was the necessary preliminary to sale or lease of land to farmers. Rombout was divided in 1708, Hyde Park in 1730, the Oblong in 1731, Lower Nine Partners in 1734, Beekman in 1737, Upper Nine Partners in 1744, Pawling in 1751, and Philipse not until 1754 (*ibid.*, pp. 58, 76, 77; Pelletreau, *Putnam County*, pp. 40-49).

36 McCracken, *Old Dutchess Forever*, p. 471. He finds only two percent of the names in the 1800 census to be Dutch.

37 Pelletreau, *Putnam County*, p. 128. The population of the region in 1790 was 8,932.

38 Journal of Abraham Rhinke, quoted in Philip Smith, *General History*, p. 112.

39 Testimony of Samuel Peters at the trial of William Prendergast, August 6, 1766. The notes on this trial, printed by Mark and Handlin, "Land Cases in Colonial New York," together with the secondary accounts of Mark, Handlin, Pelletreau, and McCracken, as previously cited, are the basis for the following paragraphs.

40 This is the judgment of Mark and Handlin, "Land Cases in Colonial New York," p. 168.

41 The Supreme Court consisted "wholly of important landowners and land speculators," the Court of Chancery was "every member . . . a large-scale landholder" (*ibid.*, pp. 118, 116).

42 Brief of Nimham (the Wappinger chieftain) before Chancery (Pelletreau, *Putnam County*, p. 79 and following; Handlin, "The Eastern Frontier of New York," p. 68).

43 *Ibid.*

44 See the testimony at the trial of Prendergast: "The reason for turning people out of possession was that those who had been turned out of possession had an equitable title but could not be defended in a course of law because they were poor . . ." (Mark and Handlin, "Land Cases in Colonial New York," pp. 175, 191). The Philipse heirs spent £2,081, 18 s., 10 d. defending their patent (Mark, *Agrarian Conflicts*, p. 150).

45 Pelletreau, *Putnam County*, pp. 105, 633-34. In the Miscellaneous Manuscripts— Dutchess County, are some "Papers left by Mr. Munroe [re]lating to Rombout patent, [Ste]phen Van Cortlandt's, Beekman's patent," including a memorandum noting "vacancies" between a number of patent boundaries. The most important boundary in dispute in 1766, that between Rombout and Philipse patents, was still unsettled in 1785 (Egbert Benson to James Duane, April 2, 1785, Duane Papers).

46 Pelletreau, *Putnam County*, pp. 633-34.

47 This and all other details are not imaginary local color, but derived from the testimony at the trial of Prendergast.

48 When Robinson was living in England in 1786, he described Prendergast as "always a saving, industrious man." Characteristically, this was in a letter to Frederick Philipse urging that the latter collect certain debts owed by Prendergast to Robinson (Robinson to Philipse, June 4, 1786, cited in Pel-

letreau, *Putnam County*, pp. 524-26).

49 In late June there were 300 tenants under arms at Quaker Hill and 1,700 at Poughkeepsie (Mark, *Agrarian Conflicts*, p. 143).

50 Handlin, "The Eastern Frontier of New York," p. 71, quoting a contemporary description.

51 William Smith, *Historical Memoirs from 12 July 1776 to 25 July 1778 of William Smith*, edited by William H. W. Sabine (New York, 1958), p. 40.

52 Handlin, "The Eastern Frontier of New York," pp. 69, 72.

53 Mark and Handlin, "Land Cases in Colonial New York," p. 167.

54 *Ibid.*, p. 169. At this time, jurymen were required to possess a ten-acre freehold (McCracken, *Old Dutchess Forever*, pp. 202-03).

55 Cadwallader Colden to the Earl of Hillsborough, April 25, 1768, in E. B. O'Callaghan, editor, *Documents Relative to the Colonial History of the State of New York* (Albany, 1856-1887), VIII, 61.

56 In 1771, Leonard Van Kleek was assessed at thirty-two pounds, Henry Livingston the next highest at thirty pounds (Platt, *Eagle's History*, p. 32).

57 Reynolds, *Eighteenth Century Records*, pp. 55, 59, 71, 72, 73, 80, 81, 96, 97, 112, 128-31, 229, 270, 283.

58 White, *Beekmans of New York*, p. 206.

59 Namier, *Structure of Politics*, p. 71. The next year, 1769, Judge Robert Livingston ran with one of the Rhinebeck Hoffmans, but was defeated again.

60 Quoted by Mark, *Agrarian Conflicts*, p. 159.

61 "A Packet of Old Letters," p. 36 n.

62 Platt, *Eagle's History*, p. 33. The diary of William Smith informs us that there was considerable pushing and pulling between the new assemblymen and the landlords over these appointments. For May 24, 1769, he writes: "The Members last winter offered a roll [i.e., a list of appointees] and Judge Livingston another some time before." For November 20 of the same year: "James Livingston the Sheriff of Dutchess was removed at the request of the Members and Justices of that county." On March 1, 1774, Smith writes: "Fanning the private Secretary told me a few days ago that Brinckerhoff the Member had applied for a new roll for Dutchess and therefore he thought he would vote for the £5000 to the Governor." And September 29, 1774: "several new Justices made at the request of Beverly Robinson in Dutchess" (*Historical Memoirs from 16 March 1763 to 9 July 1776 of William Smith*, edited by William H. W. Sabine [New York, 1956], I, 52, 68, 171-72, 193).

63 He who doubts that the American Revolution was a social movement should consider the men who replaced Livingston and Robinson as sheriff and chief judge: Melancton Smith and Ephraim Paine.

Smith was born in Long Island in 1744 and sent to Poughkeepsie to be "placed in a retail store." He was one of the few Revolutionary leaders in Dutchess who could not put an "Esquire" after his name. This title appears in the seventeen-eighties (J. Wilson Poucher, "Melancton Smith," D.C.H.S., *Yearbook*, X [1925], 39-48; "Judge M. Smith, Esq.," in J. W. Barnes to Gilbert Livingston, July 29, 1785, Gilbert Livingston Papers, Box 1).

Ephraim Paine's father was a farmer and blacksmith. Ephraim was apprenticed to a farmer as a youth, then made a modest fortune on a voyage to the West Indies. Many of his relatives were Separatist leaders, and he himself was expelled from the Senate in 1780 on the ostensible ground of being a preacher. "His integrity and firmness were not less marked than was his Puritanic simplicity of manner. He held that there should be no distinction in dress, and wore, therefore, the dress of a laboring man in the halls of legislation, and in the house of worship. Many mistakes are mentioned, resulting from Mr. Paine's plainness of dress. He was at one time treated as a menial by the landlady at whose house he was staying during his time at court in Poughkeepsie. The only rebuke he gave when she apologized was, 'you should treat all men alike.' A gentleman who rode in haste to the house on public business gave him his horse to hold while he went in to speak to Judge Paine. Another was once looking over the farm for Judge Paine, and, finding a man ditching, asked him, 'Where is your Master?' 'In Heaven,' was his ready answer. Judge Paine's education had been without the aid of schools . . . he opposed decidedly the financial policy of General Hamilton" (Newton Reed, *The Early History of Amenia* [Amenia, 1875], pp. 72, 102-03; Philip Smith, *General History*, pp. 121-22).

64 Gilbert Livingston to Robert G. Livingston, September 28, 1773, Gilbert Livingston Papers, Box 1.

65 Robinson to Duane, September 9, 1766, Duane Papers.

66 Robinson to Duane, May 8, 1772, March 25 and May 8, 1773, *ibid.*

67 Quoted by Mark, *Agrarian Conflicts*, p. 13.

68 Letter of December 5, 1775, *Journal of the Provincial Congress, Provincial Convention, Committee of Safety and Council of Safety of the State of New York* (Albany, 1842), II, 106.

CHAPTER IV

1 "Only let the farm year to year because I will sell them both as soon as possible"; "If any body would be in earnest about it I would agree about the price for I had better sell them almost at any rate than to have them out for they want repairs" (Robert G. Livingston to Gilbert Livingston, April 6, 1773, and March 22, 1775, Gilbert Livingston Papers, Box 1).

2 McCracken, *Old Dutchess Forever*, p. 224.

3 Allan Nevins, *The American States During and After the Revolution, 1775-1789* (New York, 1924), p. 268.

4 Spaulding, *New York, 1783-1789*, p. 122. It is interesting to keep in mind the significance of confiscated lands in other revolutions. Marc Bloch writes of the French Revolution: "Consider the problem of the land confiscated during the Revolution. During the Terror, and reversing the earlier legislation, the government decided to sell it off in small lots without competitive bidding . . . [What was it the men of the Year III hoped for?] Primarily, they hoped to favor the acquisition of the land by the little people of the rural areas . . . they sought the relief of the poor peasants, as a guarantee of their fidelity to the new order" (*The Historian's Craft* [New York, 1953], p. 141). And Maurice Dobb on the English Commonwealth: "It is remarkable what strong

opposition was shown . . . not only by the House of Lords, but by the Presbyterian section in the Commons, and in particular by the leading merchants who composed the common council of the City of London, to the proposed sequestration of the estates of royalists and of bishops, and to the organized sale of delinquents' lands after sequestration had already been decided upon" (*Studies in the Development of Capitalism* [London, 1947], p. 172).

5 Force, *American Archives*, Series 4, II, 304.

6 *Ibid.*

7 *Ibid.*, pp. 304-05.

8 *Ibid.*

9 Hough, *The New York Civil List*, pp. 62-65.

10 Force, *American Archives*, Series 4, I, 702; II, 304. Philip Smith, *General History*, p. 52. For what it may signify, the popular vote on the Constitution in 1788 was numerically identical with the figures for signers and nonsigners of the Association: 1,800 to 900 in each case (for the latter, see Force, *American Archives*, Series 4, III, 597-607).

11 *Ibid.*, Series 4, II, 834-35; Becker, *History of Political Parties*, p. 227.

12 McCracken, *Old Dutchess Forever*, p. 419. The draft of the 1777 constitution in the Abraham Yates Papers, New York Public Library, requires of an elector of assemblymen only that he be over twenty-one, a freeholder, a resident, and a taxpayer. Most significantly, future Anti-Federalists Gilbert Livingston and Zephaniah Platt voted for a twenty-pound freehold requirement for Assembly electors, and against making the secret ballot obligatory after the war; they joined Robert R. Livingston on both these divisions (*Journal of the Provincial Congress*, I, 867, 891-92).

13 Hough, *The New York Civil List*, pp. 62-65.

14 Jay, DeWitt, Platt, Cantine, and Tappen to George Clinton, June 2, 1777 (George Clinton, *Public Papers of George Clinton* [New York and Albany, 1899], I, 855-56).

15 Dutchess voted for Clinton 206-132, but this vote may have included many refugees from southern New York. Professor Alfred Young of Paterson State College kindly provided me with these returns.

16 James Duane to Robert R. Livingston, June 7, 1775, Livingston-Redmond Manuscripts, New York Public Library, quoted by Beverly McAnear, "Mr. Robert R. Livingston's Reasons Against A Land Tax," *Journal of Political Economy*, XLVIII (February 1940), 76.

17 Swartwout was a near neighbor of Brinckerhoff's, second to him in responsibility for the Rombout Committee of Safety, and one of the executors of his will (Reynolds, *Eighteenth Century Records*, p. 89).

18 Philip Smith, *General History*, Appendix A, pp. 477-81. Listings of rank must be used with care because men changed their rank so often.

19 Force, *American Archives*, Series 5, I, 355-57.

20 Johnson, *Colonel Henry Luddington*, p. 62. This source provides a good picture of the organization of the militia in Dutchess.

21 *Journal of the Provincial Congress*, II, 279.

22 Johnson, *Colonel Henry Luddington*, p. 95.

23 Luddington to Clinton, February 20, 1778, quoted in *ibid.*, p. 107.

24 *Ibid.*, p. 178.

25 "General Jacobus Swartwout," p. 68.

26 Johnson, *Colonel Henry Luddington*, p. 141.

27 Benton, *Troutbeck*, pp. 14-15. It is important to keep in mind that there was a great deal of both active Toryism and Whig discontent in Dutchess. For the former, see George Dangerfield, *Chancellor Robert R. Livingston of New York, 1746-1813* (New York, 1960), pp. 57, 60, 81, 87, and the manuscripts therein cited; Clinton, *Public Papers*, VI, 126, 576-77. It is often said that the tenant rioters were Tories but, judging from the contemporary references to Tory activity and from the geographic distribution of the nonsigners of the Association, I am not sure of this. Of course, "Toryism" and "Whig discontent" are elastic terms and one shaded off into the other.

28 *Journal of the Provincial Congress*, II, 355.

29 Robert R. Livingston mentions a committee to regulate prices in Albany County as early as August 1777: "tho they have not been followed by the other counties, yet they have excited a spirit that will be troublesome" (letter to Gouverneur Morris, August 8, 1777, Robert R. Livingston Papers).

30 *New York Packet*, July 15, 1779.

31 *New York Journal and General Advertiser*, July 19, 26, 1779 (hereafter referred to as *New York Journal*).

32 *New York Packet*, September 16, 1779.

33 *New York Journal*, August 9, 1779.

34 *Ibid.*, August 16, 1779.

35 *New York Packet*, May 20, July 1, September 2, 1779.

36 *New York Journal*, January 11, February 1 and 15, 1779.

37 *Ibid.*, May 17, 1779.

38 *Ibid.*, August 9, 1779.

39 John Campbell to Theodorus Van Wyck, January 31, 1780, Papers of the Commissioners for Sequestration—Dutchess County, Folder 2, New York Historical Society. These papers, acquired by the Society in 1950, were unavailable to Spaulding, Yoshpe, and other earlier students of the disposition of Loyalist lands in New York State.

40 *Journal of the Provincial Congress*, II, 407.

41 For the steps leading up to this legislation, see Harry B. Yoshpe, *The Disposition of Loyalist Estates in the Southern District of the State of New York* (New York, 1939), pp. 13-15.

42 It was the unending headache. The items involved were "one mare and sucking colt the property of Richard Vanderburgh on the farm of Wines Manny . . . Charles Davies of Beekmans has a quantity of wheat at Elijah Townsends," etc. The goods were sold at public vendue, one precinct at a time, usually by the commissioners themselves (Papers of the Commissioners, *e.g.*, Folder 2, "Memorandum of Tory Goods"; Folder 1, "The Property of Beverly Robinson sold at vendue at the house of Peter Bogardus, Nov. 24, 1777," Hugh Rea to Commissioner Sheldon, December 10, 1777, and Commissioner Van Wyck to Commissioner Livingston, December 13, 1777). Alexander Flick, using manuscripts since destroyed by fire, states that between 1777 and 1780, £24,694 was realized from the sale of the personal property of 262 Dutchess Tories;

by May 1783, the total was £99,771 (*Loyalism in New York During the American Revolution* [New York, 1901], pp. 141-42).

43 An official in Ulster wrote to Clinton, May 8, 1778, about the work of the Ulster commissioners: "They say they have not rented any as yet, and they choose not to do it, as there is women in them, I understand the Commissioners for Dutchess County has rented such farms" (Clinton, *Public Papers*, III, 282-83).

44 The Dutchess commissioners wrote to Clinton on March 16, 1778: "Your memorialists have put numbers of well affected refugees inhabitants of this state into the possession of lands and tenements deserted by the former disaffected proprietors. As yet your memorialists have stipulated with but very few of the refugees aforesaid, what rent they shall pay for the lands and tenements they occupy. Your memorialists wish to have pointed out to them, what proportion of the highest rent they could obtain from others, for lands and tenements above described, the said refugees should pay" (*ibid.*, III, 45-46; the draft of this letter is in Papers of the Commissioners, Folder 2).

45 Egbert Benson, whom the commissioners consulted on doubtful points of law, wrote to Commissioner Livingston on August 3, 1780: "The law has not pointed out any mode to the Commissioners for inquiring into titles, and . . . consequently possession must be to them sufficient evidence of right," except in the case of tenants "notoriously tenants only for a year or other short term and having no kind of interest in the improvements" and in the case of tenants whose leases would expire in less than a year (Papers of the Commissioners, Folder 2).

46 *Ibid.*, Folder 1.

47 Peter Heermance, chairman of the Rhinebeck Precinct committee, to the commissioners, March 10, 1778, *ibid.*, Folder 1.

48 Undated lease to Thomas Jenks of Charlotte, *ibid.*, Folder 2; *New York Journal*, April 5, 1779.

49 Van Wyck to Livingston, June 30, 1779, Papers of the Commissioners, Folder 1.

50 Van Wyck to Livingston, June 5 and 6, 1779, *ibid.*, Folder 1; *New York Journal*, January 11, 1779.

51 Papers of the Commissioners, Folder 1.

52 Lawrence Papers, New York Historical Society.

53 Rea to Sheldon, December 10, 1777, Papers of the Commissioners, Folder 1.

54 Van Wyck to James Cox, January 26, 1779, *ibid.*, Folder 1.

55 High taxes were, of course, another grievance. "Our county is in a pitiful situation with respect to the excise," Ephraim Paine wrote to Robert R. Livingston, February 12, 1779 (Robert R. Livingston Papers). Closely allied was quartermasters' requisitioning of crops without payment save for valueless government certificates (Livingston to John Penn, January 28, 1780, *ibid.*). For a summary of grievances see Livingston to George Washington, January 8, 1781, *ibid.*

56 See the letter of Henry Livingston at the head of this chapter; the experience of Robert G. Livingston, note 81, below; and Robert R. Livingston to the trustees of Kingston, March 1, 1778: ". . . the disaffection of my tenants who have during this controversy very generally withheld their rents" (Robert R. Livingston Papers).

57 Johnson, *Colonel Henry Luddington*, pp. 153-56. Meanwhile, Robert R. Livingston was urging Gouverneur Morris to attend the Assembly because dangerous plans were afoot to forfeit estates and give land to the soldiers (letter of September 10, 1778, Robert R. Livingston Papers).

58 New York Assembly Papers, XXVI, New York State Library.

59 Livingston to Van Wyck, March 31, 1780, Papers of the Commissioners, Folder 2. Actually, only the lands of a certain number of Loyalists formally attainted were sold. With respect to the farms of other, less prominent Loyalists, a trickle of leasing continued: The Dutchess commissioners leased twenty-eight farms from March 16 to May 24, 1782, and thirty-eight farms from February to November, 1783 (*ibid.*, Folder 2, Farms Leased by the Commissioners of Sequestration).

60 Letter of March 4, 1779, Robert R. Livingston Papers.

61 *Votes and Proceedings of the Assembly of the State of New York* (Fishkill, 1779), pp. 26, 28.

62 Tillotson to Livingston, December 13, 1779, and Margaret Beekman Livingston to Livingston, December 30, 1779, Robert R. Livingston Papers. Two-and-a-half years later, Mrs. Livingston was still complaining about DeWitt's assessments. By that time he was also rating her for the Dutchess poor tax (Margaret Beekman Livingston to Robert R. Livingston, July 16, 1782, *ibid.*).

63 George Clinton to Robert R. Livingston, January 7, 1780; Philip Schuyler to same, February 18, 1780; Margaret Beekman Livingston to same, February 1780; John Sloss Hobart to same, February 15, 1780 (*ibid.*); for the weather, *New York Journal*, January 10 and February 21, 1780. Two years later the contractor Jacob Cuyler wrote to James Duane about his services in "seventy nine eighty when they were ready to disband for the want of provisions" (Duane Papers). See also Dangerfield, *Chancellor Robert R. Livingston*, p. 119: "The winter of 1779-1780, in the annals of the northern army, was perhaps even more fearful than the one that had seen it freezening and sickening at Valley Forge."

64 *Votes and Proceedings of the Assembly of the State of New York* (Albany, 1780), p. 95.

65 *Ibid.*, pp. 105, 112, 113.

66 This was not a contest of "good guys" and "bad guys." On February 25 a bill was introduced providing that slaves who voluntarily enlisted for three years with the consent of their masters should be free from the time of enlistment. Brinckerhoff moved to reject, supported by Sackett; Benson voted in favor. Of 5,941 persons in Brinckerhoff's home precinct of Rombout in 1790, 601 were slaves (Reynolds, *Eighteenth Century Records*, p. 7).

67 *Votes and Proceedings* (1780), pp. 122, 129.

68 *Ibid.*, p. 150. A rejection by the Council of Revision had been overridden on March 8 with far more than the requisite two-thirds majority, all the Dutchess delegates voting together. Again the name of James Jay stands out among the tiny minority (*ibid.*, pp. 144-45).

69 Hamilton later called Benson the preeminent figure in the New York Assembly during the Revolution (writing as "H—G—" in the *New York Daily Advertiser*, March 12, 1789). In a letter Walter Livingston wrote to Robert R. Livingston on January 7, 1781, he referred to Benson as one who "is supposed to

govern the politics of this State" (Robert R. Livingston Papers).

[70] Livingston to Jay, April 20, 1779; Benson to Livingston, March 20, 1780, *ibid.* See also Benson's explanation to Livingston of why he would support price regulation (letter of January 3, 1780, *ibid.*). Hobart, on the other hand, acquiesced in the sale of lands as "the offspring of dire necessity" but said of regulation, "I shall oppose that hydra to the last"; a third Federalist-to-be, Tillotson, also opposed price regulation (Hobart to Livingston, November 15, 1779, and February 15, 1780; Tillotson to Livingston, December 13, 1779, *ibid.*).

[71] Writing to Livingston after the spring elections of 1780, Benson said that all but one troublemaker of "the little faction which was found last winter" had been defeated (letters of June 28 and July 28, *ibid.*). Benson's letter of July 28 again shows him steering a middle course, this time in regard to paper money: "the tender and penal clauses are neither yours nor mine, I was obliged to consent to them or I should have lost the whole bill."

The fact that Brinckerhoff and Sackett, the two Dutchess representatives who favored the confiscation and sale of Loyalist estates in every division in the Assembly of 1779-1780, were the two who also lost their seats in the 1780 election suggests that they may have been among the objects of the conservative "purge." On April 20, 1779, Livingston had written to Jay: "many preparatory steps were taken to produce a change in the delegations which will take effect shortly" (*ibid.*).

[72] Spaulding, *New York, 1783-1789*, p. 52.

[73] On March 15, 1785, the Assembly defeated a proposal to continue this aspect of the law. Brinckerhoff and Mathew Patterson (also of south Dutchess) voted with the minority (*Votes and Proceedings of the Assembly of the State of New York* [New York, 1785], p. 90).

[74] On March 27, 1781, the Assembly voted on whether to give tenants four or eight months in which to apply for their right of preemption. It is interesting to find Jacobus Swartwout voting with Benson for the shorter term. Of the Dutchess delegation only Dodge, who as a commissioner may have had a first-hand appreciation of the human consequences of the bill, voted for the longer term. Brinckerhoff either was not present or did not vote (*Votes and Proceedings of the Assembly of the State of New York* [for the year 1781; Albany, 1820], p. 86).

[75] Yoshpe, *Disposition of Loyalist Estates*, pp. 20-21.

[76] The most recent studies are, for the Southern District of New York, *ibid.*, and for the north and western part of the state, Catherine Snell Crary, "Forfeited Loyalist Lands in the Western District of New York: Albany and Tyron Counties," *New York History*, XXV (July 1954), 239-58. Forfeited lands in the Middle District, which included Dutchess County, have never been studied.

[77] Yoshpe, *Disposition of Loyalist Estates*, pp. 50-63, demonstrates that many tenants on the Philipse Manor in Westchester purchased their farms. E. Wilder Spaulding points out that Yoshpe rather slights his own Westchester evidence when he concludes that "patriotic profiteers contrived to get the bulk of the loyalist estates into their own hands" (review of Harry B. Yoshpe, *The Disposition of Loyalist Estates in the Southern District of the State of New*

York, in *American Historical Review,* XLV [July 1940], 899-900; Yoshpe, *Disposition of Loyalist Estates,* p. 115).

78 Except where indicated, the facts on this page are derived from the Abstract of Forfeited Lands for Dutchess County, New York Historical Society. This volume consists of abstracts of deeds and corresponds exactly to Ledger A of Deeds in the county records at Poughkeepsie. It was compiled by the three Dutchess commissioners for selling the forfeited lands and is signed by them.

79 The tax list is printed in Pelletreau, *Putnam County,* pp. 122-28.

80 *New York Journal,* July 24, 1780.

81 Pelletreau, *Putnam County,* p. 93.

82 Abstract of Forfeited Lands, pp. 27, 28, 43-44, 44-45, 70-71, 99, 107, 133.

83 The plight of the indigent tenant who could not afford to buy his land is suggested by the following petition, dated January 15, 1781: "We the subscribers beg leave to represent the circumstance of Daniel Hunt who is now eighty-seven years of age. He lives on a small farm that did belong to Col. Robinson not more than twenty acres of improved land. He has always been friendly to the country he has lived on the place twelve years. If you will be pleased to order that the place may not be sold but let him continue the few days he has to live it can't be long and he is not able to buy it. If he is turned off he must be a precinct charge . . ." (Miscellaneous Manuscripts—Dutchess County).

Another way in which a tenant might lose control of his farm is illustrated by the speculator, William Duer, arriving at an auction of Dutchess forfeited lands too late to bid and buying two farms from previous purchasers (East, *Business Enterprise,* p. 112).

84 Yoshpe, *Disposition of Loyalist Estates,* p. 56.

85 Henry G. Livingston to Gilbert Livingston, March 4, 1781, Gilbert Livingston Papers, Box 1.

86 Spaulding presents price series on both wheat and bread which he interprets to show a rise in price between 1785 and 1788 (*New York, 1783-1789,* pp. 18-19); but a later study (Arthur Harrison Cole, *Wholesale Commodity Prices in the United States, 1700-1861* [Cambridge, 1938], pp. 79, 84-85, 87-88) presents series on beef, pork, and wheat which steadily decrease throughout the decade. Spaulding definitely confuses increased production with agricultural prosperity (*New York, 1783-1789,* pp. 23-24). Actually, bumper crops would have sent the price on down.

87 Robert G. Livingston to Gilbert Livingston, November 22, 1786: "Please to send the enclosed letter to Enoch Lester, he lives on the farm of Benjamin Lester, he told me when I saw him that he would purchase my mortgage. If you should see tell him he must either buy it or pay rent for future" (Gilbert Livingston Papers, Box 1).

88 "In the spring of 1788 the press of New York City, Poughkeepsie and Albany printed more notices of insolvencies and sales of mortgaged property than in the previous year" (Spaulding, *New York, 1783-1789,* p. 21).

89 Volumes XXV, XXVI.

90 New York Senate Papers, X, Box 2; XI, Box 1, New York State Library.

91 Frederick C. Haacker, *Early Settlers of Putnam County, New York* (typescript, New York State Library, 1946), p. 2.

[92] McCracken, *Old Dutchess Forever*, p. 425.

[93] *New York Journal*, March 15 and 22, 1779.

[94] Philip Smith, *General History*, p. 240.

[95] Zimm, *Southeastern New York*, p. 383.

[96] H. W. Reynolds, "The Story of Dutchess County," D.C.H.S., *Yearbook*, XVIII (1933), 32; to the same effect, McCracken, *Old Dutchess Forever*, pp. 425, 430, 433.

[97] David Maldwyn Ellis, *Landlords and Farmers in the Hudson-Mohawk Region, 1790-1850* (Ithaca, 1946), p. 28; to the same effect, Spaulding, *New York, 1783-1789*, p. 6. The electoral census of 1790 lists 1,115 tenants in Dutchess.

[98] Henry G. Livingston to Gilbert Livingston, August 1, 1782, Gilbert Livingston Papers, Box 1.

[99] *New York Journal*, January 4, August 16, 1779; *New York Packet*, August 19, September 2, 1779.

[100] "If I take the oath before a Justice will it answer?" (Henry G. Livingston to Gilbert Livingston, October 15, 1782, Gilbert Livingston Papers, Box 1).

[101] Robert G. Livingston to Gilbert Livingston, October 26, 1785, *ibid.*, Box I.

[102] Henry G. Livingston to Gilbert Livingston, February 1, 1785, *ibid.*, Box I.

[103] McCracken, *Old Dutchess Forever*, p. 442.

[104] Livingston to Morris, January 18, 1781; Livingston to Washington, January 8, 1781, Robert R. Livingston Papers.

[105] Margaret Beekman Livingston to Robert R. Livingston, December 22, 1781, *ibid.*

[106] Tillotson to Livingston, June 17, 1782, *ibid.*

[107] St. Jean de Crevecoeur, *Letters from an American Farmer* (New York, 1904), pp. 52-55.

[108] *Ibid.*, pp. 77, 79.

CHAPTER V

[1] *Country Journal*, July 29, 1788.

[2] See Lansing's remarks on July 24 beginning, "The gentleman from Dutchess promised to bring forward a motion . . ." (Gilbert Livingston convention notes, Gilbert Livingston Papers).

[3] Ezra Thompson, the seventh Dutchess delegate, did not vote.

[4] Debates of July 12, 15, 17, 18, Gilbert Livingston Papers and McKesson Papers, New York Historical Society.

[5] *New York Daily Advertiser*, July 28, 1788; and the letter of the New York City Anti-Federalists to the Anti-Federalists of other counties, November 4, 1788, drafted by Smith, Lamb, and Hughes (Lamb Papers, Box 5).

[6] Debates of July 25, Gilbert Livingston Papers.

[7] Debates of June 21, Jonathan Eliot, editor, *Debates in the Several State Conventions on the Adoption of the Federal Constitution* (Philadelphia, 1896), II, 244-48.

[8] Debates of June 23, *ibid.*, II, 281.

[9] *Ibid.*, II, 277.

[10] *Ibid.*

11 Like the "Captain Swartwout" of the letter, Jacobus Swartwout was a captain and lived on the land claimed by Catherine Brett ("General Jacobus Swartwout," D.C.H.S., *Yearbook*, XIII [1928], 67).

12 Brett to Johnson, August 26, 1762 (McCracken, *Old Dutchess Forever*, pp. 278-79).

13 Quoted by Pelletreau, *Putnam County*, p. 71.

14 "Travelled Documents," D.C.H.S., *Yearbook*, XX (1935), 87.

15 Mark and Handlin, "Land Cases in Colonial New York," p. 193.

16 As does Louis Hartz, *The Liberal Tradition in America* (New York, 1955), Chapter 3.

BIBLIOGRAPHY

1 MANUSCRIPTS

Abraham Yates Papers. New York Public Library.
Abstract of Forfeited Lands for Dutchess County. New York Historical Society.
Bancroft Transcripts. New York Public Library.
Duane Papers. New York Historical Society.
Gilbert Livingston Land Papers. New York Public Library.
Gilbert Livingston Papers. New York Public Library.
Henry Livingston Papers. Franklin Delano Roosevelt Library: Hyde Park.
Lamb Papers. New York Historical Society.
Lawrence and Smith Papers. New York Historical Society.
Lawrence Papers. New York Historical Society.
Ledger A of Deeds. Dutchess County Clerk's Office, Poughkeepsie.
McKesson Papers. New York Historical Society.

Miscellaneous Manuscripts—Dutchess County. New York Historical Society.

New York Assembly Papers, XXV, XXVI. New York State Library.

New York Senate Papers, X, Box 2; XI, Box 1. New York State Library.

Papers of the Commissioners for Sequestration—Dutchess County. New York Historical Society.

Robert R. Livingston Papers. New York Historical Society.

Supervisors' Records, 1771-1785, 1786-1794. Dutchess County Clerk's Office, Poughkeepsie.

Tax Lists, 1771-1779. Adriance Memorial Library, Poughkeepsie.

W.P.A. Inventory of Dutchess County Records. Franklin Delano Roosevelt Library, Hyde Park.

2 DOCUMENTS, PROCEEDINGS, RECORDS

Clinton, George. *Public Papers of George Clinton.* 10 vols. New York and Albany, 1899.

Eliot, Jonathan, editor. *Debates in the Several State Conventions on the Adoption of the Federal Constitution.* 5 vols. Philadelphia, 1896.

Force, Peter, editor. *American Archives.* Series 4, 6 vols. Washington, 1837.

Heads of Families at the First Census of the United States Taken in the Year 1790—New York. Washington, 1908.

Journal of the Provincial Congress, Provincial Convention, Committee of Safety and Council of Safety of the State of New York. 2 vols. Albany, 1842.

O'Callaghan, E. B., editor. *Documentary History of the State of New York.* 4 vols. Albany, 1851.

——— *Documents Relative to the Colonial History of the State of New York.* 15 vols. Albany, 1856-1887.

Reynolds, Helen Wilkinson, editor. *Eighteenth Century Records of the Portion of Dutchess County, New York, that was included in Rombout Precinct.* Dutchess County Historical Society, Collections, VI. Poughkeepsie, 1938.

Roosevelt, Franklin Delano, editor. *Records of Crum Elbow Precinct, Dutchess County, New York, 1738-1761, together with Records of Charlotte Precinct, 1762-1785, Records of Clinton Precinct, 1786-1788 and Records of the Town of Clinton, 1789-1799.* Dutchess County Historical Society, Collections, VII. Poughkeepsie, 1940.

Smith, William. *Historical Memoirs from 16 March 1763 to 9 July 1776 of William Smith,* edited by William H. W. Sabine. New York, 1956.

———— *Historical Memoirs from 12 July 1776 to 25 July 1778 of William Smith,* edited by William H. W. Sabine. New York, 1958.

Votes and Proceedings of the Assembly of the State of New York, 1779-1785. Various places and dates.

3   NEWSPAPERS

Country Journal and Poughkeepsie Advertiser. Poughkeepsie.
New York Daily Advertiser. New York City.
New York Journal and General Advertiser. Poughkeepsie.
New York Packet. Fishkill.

4   SECONDARY AUTHORITIES

A   *Works Dealing with the Ratification Struggle in Other States and in the Nation as a Whole*

Beard, Charles A. *An Economic Interpretation of the Constitution of the United States.* New York, 1913.

Benson, Lee. "A Critique of Beard and his Critics." Unpublished.

Brown, Robert E. *Charles Beard and the Constitution: A Critical Analysis of "An Economic Interpretation of the Constitution."* Princeton, 1956.

——— *Middle-Class Democracy and the Revolution in Massachusetts, 1691-1780.* Ithaca, 1955.

Crowl, Philip A. "Anti-Federalism in Maryland, 1787-1788." *William and Mary Quarterly*, 3d series, IV (October 1947), 446-69.

Handlin, Oscar and Mary. "Radicals and Conservatives in Massachusetts after Independence." *New England Quarterly*, XVII (September 1944), 343-55.

Hofstadter, Richard. "Beard and the Constitution: The History of an Idea." Reprint from *American Quarterly*, II (Fall 1950).

Jameson, J. F., editor. *Essays in the Constitutional History of the United States in the Formative Period, 1775-1789.* Baltimore, 1889.

Jensen, Merrill. *The Articles of Confederation.* Madison, 1940.

——— *The New Nation: A History of the United States During the Confederation, 1781-1789.* New York, 1950.

Kenyon, Cecilia M. "Men of Little Faith: The Anti-Federalists on the Nature of Representative Government." *William and Mary Quarterly*, 3d series, XII (January 1955), 3-43.

Libby, Oran. "The Geographical Distribution of the Vote of the Thirteen States on the Federal Constitution, 1787-8." *Bulletin of the University of Wisconsin: Economics, Political Science, and History*, Series I. Madison, 1897.

McDonald, Forrest. *We, The People: The Economic Origins of the Constitution.* Chicago, 1958.

Main, Jackson T. "Charles A. Beard and the Constitution: A Critical Review of Forrest McDonald's *We, The People*." *William and Mary Quarterly*, 3d series, XVII (January 1960), 86-102.

——— "Sections and Politics in Virginia, 1781-1787." *Wil-*

112

liam and Mary Quarterly, 3d series, XII (January 1955), 96-112.

Morgan, Edmund S. "The American Revolution: Revisions in Need of Revising." *William and Mary Quarterly*, 3d series, XIV (January 1957), 3-15.

Morris, Richard B. "The Confederation Period and the American Historian." *William and Mary Quarterly*, 3d series, XIII (April 1956), 139-56.

Thomas, Robert E. "The Virginia Convention of 1778: A Criticism of Beard's *An Economic Interpretation of the Constitution*." *Journal of Southern History*, XIX (February 1953), 63-72.

B   *Works Dealing with New York State*

Aly, Bower. *The Rhetoric of Alexander Hamilton*. New York, 1941.

Barrett, Walter. *The Old Merchants of New York City*. 5 vols. New York, 1885.

Becker, Carl L. *The History of Political Parties in the Province of New York, 1760-1776*. Madison, 1909.

Cochran, Thomas C. *New York in the Confederation: An Economic Study*. Philadelphia, 1932.

Crary, Catherine Snell. "Forfeited Loyalist Lands in the Western District of New York: Albany and Tryon Counties." *New York History*, XXV (July 1954), 239-58.

Dangerfield, George. *Chancellor Robert R. Livingston of New York, 1746-1813*. New York, 1960.

East, Robert A. *Business Enterprise in the American Revolutionary Era*. New York, 1938.

Ellis, David Maldwyn. *Landlords and Farmers in the Hudson-Mohawk Region, 1790-1850*. Ithaca, 1946.

———— "The Yankee Invasion of New York, 1783-1850." *New York History*, XXXII (January 1951), 3-17.

Flick, Alexander. *Loyalism in New York during the American Revolution.* New York, 1901.

Flick, Alexander, editor. *The American Revolution in New York.* Albany, 1926.

Fox, Dixon Ryan. *The Decline of Aristocracy in the Politics of New York.* New York, 1919.

Haacker, Frederick C. *Early Settlers of Putnam County, New York.* Typescript. New York State Library, 1946.

Horton, John Theodore. *James Kent: A Study in Conservatism, 1763-1847.* New York, 1939.

Hough, Franklin B. *The New York Civil List.* Albany, 1861.

Klein, Milton M. "Democracy and Politics in Colonial New York." *New York History,* XL (July 1959), 221-46.

Leake, Isaac. *Memoir of the Life and Times of General John Lamb.* Albany, 1850.

McAnear, Beverly. "Mr. Robert R. Livingston's Reasons Against A Land Tax." *Journal of Political Economy,* XLVIII (February 1940), 63-90.

Mark, Irving. *Agrarian Conflict in Colonial New York, 1711-1775.* New York, 1940.

Mason, Bernard. "Organization of the Revolutionary Movement in New York State, 1775-1777." Unpublished Ph.d. thesis, Columbia University, 1958.

Miner, Clarence E. *The Ratification of the Federal Constitution by the State of New York.* New York, 1921.

Nevins, Allan. *The American States During and After the Revolution, 1775-1789.* New York, 1924.

Petrie, Robert G. "Sectionalism and Self-Interest in the Struggle for the Constitution in New York State." Unpublished Master's thesis, Columbia University, 1954.

Spaulding, E. Wilder. *His Excellency George Clinton: Critic of the Constitution.* New York, 1938.

———— *New York in the Critical Period, 1783-1789.* New York, 1932.

Spaulding, E. Wilder. "The Ratification of the Federal Consti-
tution." In Alexander Flick, editor, *History of the State of
New York*, V, 29-64. New York, 1934.
——— Review of Harry B. Yoshpe, *The Disposition of Loyalist
Estates in the Southern District of the State of New York.*
In *American Historical Review*, XLV (July 1940), 899-
900.
Spencer, Charles W. "Sectional Aspects of New York Provincial
Politics." *Political Science Quarterly*, XXX (September
1915), 397-424.
Troy (New York) Times. *The Past and Present of Plattsburgh.*
Troy, 1891.
Wolos, Jacob. "The Land Situation in New York, 1750-1775."
Unpublished Master's thesis, Columbia University, 1927.
Yoshpe, Harry B. "The Delancey Estate: Did the Revolution
Democratize Landholding in New York?" *New York His-
tory*, XVII (April 1936), 167-79.
——— *The Disposition of Loyalist Estates in the Southern Dis-
trict of the State of New York.* New York, 1939.
Zeichner, Oscar. "The Loyalist Problem in New York after the
Revolution." *New York History*, XXI (July 1940), 284-
302.

c   *Works Dealing with Dutchess County*

Bayne, Martha Collins. *County at Large.* Poughkeepsie, 1937.
Benton, Charles E. *Troutbeck: A Dutchess County Homestead.*
Poughkeepsie, 1916.
Desmond, Alice Curtis. "Mary Philipse: Heiress." *New York
History*, XXVIII (January 1947), 22-32.
Dutchess County Historical Society. *Yearbook.* Various dates.
Federal Writers' Project American Guide Series. *Dutchess
County.* Philadelphia, 1937.
Gordon, Joan. "Kinship and Class: The Livingstons of New
York, 1675-1860." Unpublished Ph.d. thesis, Columbia

University, 1959.

Handlin, Oscar. "The Eastern Frontier of New York." *New York History*, XVIII (January 1937), 50-75.

Hasbrouck, Frank, editor. *The History of Dutchess County, New York*. Poughkeepsie, 1909.

Historical and Genealogical Record, Dutchess and Putnam Counties, New York. Poughkeepsie, 1912.

Huntting, Isaac. *History of Little Nine Partners of North East Precinct, and Pine Plains, New York*. 2 vols. Amenia, 1897.

Johnson, Willis Fletcher. *Colonel Henry Luddington: A Memoir*. New York, 1907.

Kinkead, George B. "Gilbert Livingston and Some of his Descendants." *New York Genealogical and Biographical Record*, LXXXIV (1953) and LXXXVI (1955).

McCracken, Henry Noble. *Old Dutchess Forever! The Story of an American County*. New York, 1956.

Maher, Richard Francis. *Historic Dover*. Poughkeepsie, 1908.

Mark, Irving and Oscar Handlin. "Land Cases in Colonial New York, 1765-1767: The King vs. William Prendergast." *New York University Law Review*, XIX (January 1942), 165-94.

Pelletreau, William S. *History of Putnam County, New York*. Philadelphia, 1886.

Platt, Edmund. *The Eagle's History of Poughkeepsie from the Earliest Settlement, 1683-1905*. Poughkeepsie, 1905.

Reed, Newton. *The Early History of Amenia*. Amenia, 1875.

Smith, James H. *History of Dutchess County, New York*. Syracuse, 1882.

Smith, Philip H. *General History of Dutchess County from 1609 to 1876 Inclusive*. New York, 1877.

Smith, Richard. *A Tour of Four Great Rivers: The Hudson, Mohawk, Susquehanna and Delaware in 1769*, edited by Francis W. Halsey. New York, 1906.

116

Stearns, Amanda Akin. *Ancient Homes and Early Days of Quaker Hill.* Quaker Hill, 1903.

White, Philip L. *The Beekmans of New York in Politics and Commerce, 1647-1877.* New York, 1956.

Wilson, Warren H. *Quaker Hill: A Sociological Study.* New York, 1907.

Zimm, Louise Hasbrouck and others, editors. *Southeastern New York: A History of the Counties of Ulster, Dutchess, Orange, Rockland and Putnam.* 3 vols. New York, 1946.

INDEX

ACKNOWLEDGMENTS

We would like to acknowledge the permission of the following publishers to use quoted material from their publications.

Colburn and Tegg for quoted passages from *Historical Memoirs from 16 March 1763 to 9 July 1776 of William Smith*, edited by William H. W. Sabine.

Columbia University Press for the quoted passage from *The Disposition of Loyalist Estates in the Southern District of the State of New York* by Harry B. Yoshpe.

Dutchess County Historical Society for quoted passages from their *Yearbook*.

Institute of Early American History and Culture for the quoted passage from the *William and Mary Quarterly*, the article entitled "Sections and Politics in Virginia, 1781-1787" by Jackson Main.

Alfred A. Knopf, Inc. for the quoted passage from *The Historian's Craft* by Marc Bloch.

125

Henry Noble McCracken for the quoted passages from his book *Old Dutchess Forever!* published by Hastings House, Publishers, Inc.

The Macmillan Company for the quoted passages from *An Economic Interpretation of the Constitution of the United States* by Charles Beard.

New York State Historical Association for the quoted passage from *New York History*, the article entitled "The Eastern Frontier of New York" by Oscar Handlin.

Routledge and Kegan Paul, Ltd. for the quoted passage from *Studies in the Development of Capitalism* by Maurice Dobb.

University of Chicago Press for the quoted passage from the *Journal of Political Economy*, the article entitled "Mr. Robert R. Livingston's Reasons Against A Land Tax" by Beverly McAnear; and the passage from *We, the People: The Economic Origins of the Constitution* by Forrest McDonald.

University of Wisconsin Press for the quoted passage from *The Articles of Confederation; an Interpretation of the Social-Constitutional History of the American Revolution, 1774-1781* by Merrill Jensen; and the passage from *The History of Political Parties in the Province of New York, 1760-1776* by Carl L. Becker.

About this book

Anti-Federalism in Dutchess County, New York was designed by William Nicoll of EDIT, INC. It was set in the composing room of TAMWILL CORPORATION. The text is 12 on 14 Bodoni Book; the reduced matter, 10 on 12; and the notes, 8 on 10. The display type is 12 Bodoni Book caps.

It was printed by PHOTOPRESS, INC. on WARREN'S 60-pound English Finish paper and bound by A. C. ENGDAHL AND COMPANY, INC. in BANCROFT cloth.